K.I.S.S. (Keep It Simple & Sexy)

SHEEBA FORBES

KEEP IT SIMPLE
& SEXY

The Career Guide for Women
Unwilling to Compromise

NEW YORK

LONDON • NASHVILLE • MELBOURNE • VANCOUVER

K.I.S.S. (Keep It Simple & Sexy)

The Career Guide for Women Unwilling to Compromise

Published in New York, New York, by Morgan James Publishing. Morgan James is a trademark of Morgan James, LLC. www.MorganJamesPublishing.com

Morgan James BOGO™

A **FREE** ebook edition is available for you or a friend with the purchase of this print book.

CLEARLY SIGN YOUR NAME ABOVE

Instructions to claim your free ebook edition:
1. Visit MorganJamesBOGO.com
2. Sign your name CLEARLY in the space above
3. Complete the form and submit a photo of this entire page
4. You or your friend can download the ebook to your preferred device

ISBN 9781631953996 paperback
ISBN 9781631954009 eBook
Library of Congress Control Number:
2020949674

Cover Design by:
Megan Dillon
megan@creativeninjadesigns.com

Interior Design by:
Christopher Kirk
www.GFSstudio.com

Morgan James PUBLISHING Builds with... Habitat for Humanity®
Peninsula and Greater Williamsburg

Morgan James is a proud partner of Habitat for Humanity Peninsula and Greater Williamsburg. Partners in building since 2006.

Get involved today! Visit
MorganJamesPublishing.com/giving-back

To Steven Williams, former client & CEO, of Suncor Energy and Petro Canada Inc. The memory of Stanley Herbert Hartt, a dear friend, advisor, and Chairman of my Board. My precious children, Jared and Sage who affirm for me the true meaning of life and success. I love you both so very much!

And mostly, this book is dedicated to God, from whom all good things flow.

TABLE OF CONTENTS

ACKNOWLEDGMENTS

give a huge shout out to Raoul Davis of The Ascendant Group. Without his vision, skill, faith, friendship, and presence in my life, this book and course would not exist. Jared, Sage, and I thank you, Raoul!

PREFACE

K.I.S.S. (Keep It Simple & Sexy): The Career Guide for Women Unwilling to Compromise, was written to show you how easy it is to incorporate your unique personality, values, and visions into a strategy for success! 'Self-awareness', aka thoughtful sophistication, aka personal mastery, aka emotional intelligence, matters. With it, we are better able to understand, tap into, and then leverage the amazingness of our potential. Without it, we play small, set ourselves up for disappointment, and settle for less than we deserve in our careers, relationships, and overall happiness.

The theory behind this career guide borrows from Behavioral Science, Artificial Intelligence, Metaphysics (our system of design regarding the spiritual relationship between mind and matter, appearance and substance, form and essence), established business practices, and my two decades as an accomplished executive life coach. Chalked full of real-life stories, and guided exercises you are shown how to develop an inspiring vision of success for your life and then, you are shown how to achieve it!

K.I.S.S. is a unique, inside out process for success and sexiness entirely informed by knowledge, reason, and evidence. Faith is an evidence-based function, and as such, frequent reference is made to the evidence and presence of God.

K.I.S.S. (Keep It Simple & Sexy): The Career Guide for Women Unwilling to Compromise, introduces readers to the 4-week online companion course; Self-Awareness for Success, www.mapforward.org/success.

My hope is the contents presented and packaged herein offer you lasting resonance and catapults you to fulfilling success and abundance, on your terms.

Tap into your potential, claim your Throne, and let your sexy flow!

INTRODUCTION

K.I.S.S. (*Keep It Simple & Sexy*): *The Career Guide for Women Unwilling to Compromise*, is predicated on the psychological state known as "self-awareness" — a concept that directly impacts and influences our success in life, and informs my simple formula:

Self-Awareness + Focus + Strategy = Success.

Self-awareness is informative, directional and success enabling. Each of us are required to understand our unique potential if we want to feel and be more alive. Unless and until you grasp the invisible powerful influence of your personality, your personal values, and your visions you will never realize the depth and breadth of your potential for success and sexiness. We already know that bluffing, or guessing our way through life, or doing things that others tell us we 'should' do, is unfulfilling and frustrating.

Is this book for you?

Do you know what gives you satisfaction and fulfillment?

Do you want to know how to live your potential?

Do you want to be more engaged with your life?

Are you ready for more satisfying results, success, and/or sexiness?

Are you pleased with your current reality?

Are you motivated? Are you progressing?

Do you have a standard for personal excellence?

Do you want to know IF you have the values or personality it takes to be your own boss, AND succeed?

Do you know the complimentary values to look for in your romantic relationships?

If you want answers to any of these questions, *K.I.S.S. (Keep It Simple & Sexy): The Career Guide for Women Unwilling to Compromise*, is for you!

Celebrate your potential. Get ready to thrive. You are hardwired to succeed!

This proven process, typically only a business: business offering, is the first comprehensive results-producing system being made available to the general public. The contents herein will educate, enable and empower you to claim your Throne as the Queen you are.

K.I.S.S is broken down into four parts that follow the outline of my formula:

$$Self\text{-}Awareness + Focus + Strategy = Success$$

I take you through the self-awareness, focus, and strategy elements of the formula in the first three parts, and the success element, Corporate America, in the fourth part.

K.I.S.S. is informed by science, a valid reliable form of AI technology known as a psychometric. The insights from behavioral science direct the formula, process, book, and the 4-week online course, "Self-Awareness for Success," www.mapforward.org/success. Everything you will be reading about and learning, is simple. Follow the process, learn how to play to your strengths, and set yourself up for success!

Self-awareness is a competitive advantage that builds confidence. Confidence is sexy.

WHO you are matters!

You were designed to be the star, the lead, and the Queen of your own life. Claim your Throne and live the life you deserve! You don't have to do it alone! If you want more reinforcement as you develop your amazingness, sign up for the companion 4-week online course, and journey with me and others in our community of like-minded seekers: deepen your learning, better understand your potential, and achieve better results.

The contents of this book are predicated on these three proven truths:

1. Our unique personalities are our tickets to abundance and joy
2. Our personal values are our unique success triggers
3. Visions/purpose/destiny extend directly from our personality and our values

Awaken the potential lying dormant inside of you. It's time to boldly embrace the abundance you are destined for!

K.I.S.S. mirrors my style of coaching, which is casual and informal, as though you and I are already friends; themes are often repeated to ensure retention.

You may prefer I be less repetitive, and more directional at times, however, doing so would negate your personal excellence as the creative, resourceful, and whole woman you are. A good coach focuses on the desired objectives of their client, not the specifics or details; that's your role. I acknowledge my passion, conviction, and desire to be authentic comes, at times, at the expense of grammar and punctuation; for that, I do apologize.

If you continue on this journey with me, Sheeba, your Coach, and friend, I promise to support you and help you achieve your desired results, as able. You are invited to stay in touch with me. Call me at 001–(905) 582–6030. 1 answer my own phone, if I miss your call, leave me a clear specific message and phone number; I will call you back.

I've enabled, seen, and lived the life-altering changes of this formula and process, and benefited enormously from it. I've also experienced the frustration, and loneliness of having to figure it out, on my own. In many ways, I know what you'll be going through and that is why I am making myself available. It is an easy process, and I hope that, in so far as a book can, *K.I.S.S.* helps you move forward in your life, and remains on your bedside, for years to come.

As we end this introductory chapter and proceed into Part 1, "Self-Awareness," know in advance that the journey to self-discovery for personal growth and success is stimulating, exciting, inspiring, interesting, and, sometimes lonely—all at the same time. It's also the richest journey you'll ever take.

PART 1
Self-awareness

Chapter 1
The Journey Begins...

And let me tell you, it's an exciting one! The journey forward is about finding yourself and living your purpose; understanding who you are and who you are meant to be. For these reasons and more, it is the most excellent adventure you can take: a journey, that leads you to the people, possibilities, and opportunities that complement who you are!

It matters to me that you succeed on this journey because a win for one is a win for all! If you succeed, your family, friends, strangers, your employer, your clients and customers, my children, me, and so on, also benefit—we share this world with you! This guide for career success and sexiness will hopefully enable and encourage you to lead the charge and be amongst an elite group in the world who tap into, and lead with the greatness of their potential!

Thoughtful sophistication, another term for self-awareness, is admittedly a vague concept to grasp—not unlike the subject of oxygen, the breath of life. We know oxygen is necessary to stay alive, and we know it impacts EVERYTHING. Like oxygen, self-awareness impacts EVERYTHING. That's right: EVERYTHING! There is not an aspect of your life that self-awareness, the presence or the absence thereof, does not influence. While we don't need to be self-aware to stay alive; with self-awareness, like with oxygen, the more we have of it the better life is. While oxygen just is conscious effort is required to be thoughtfully sophisticated. I hope this book helps you become more thoughtfully sophisticated, self-aware.

Life was meant to be a meaningful, rewarding, joyous opportunity for all! None of us has to be that woman who, in the absence of an informed sense of her potential, has low expectations for her life and consistently underachieves. None of us has to be that woman who, in the absence of an informed sense of her potential, sets herself up for all kinds of unnecessary avoidable risks, disappointments, and/or stresses that she may be ill-equipped to deal with. Whether we play small or are unrealistic too often, both approaches damage mental health. Thoughtful sophistication, in my experience, addresses many self-esteem and mental health issues. The more effort you make to understand yourself from the inside-out, the easier it is to see all that is loveable about you. When we can see and believe in ourselves, we confidently and successfully assimilate more with the world around us. You have more control than you realize! Plus, I am here to be your Cheerleader and Guide. If you need help organizing your power or want a reminder of your worthiness, call me. Not all of us are blessed with champions who support us and, or our potential. I would be honored to champion you and your potential! You are powerful. You can do anything you set your mind to. Betty was already 33 years of age before she realized she had potential. She had been accepting and believing what others told her about her abilities; she didn't know what else to believe. Do not take your cues from the outside world, look within, find a proven process that helps you understand your amazingness and then helps you to realize your potential. Unless you know, believe, and understand that you are worthy of a Throne, how can you claim it?

Recap:
1. Self-Awareness/Thoughtful Sophistication influences every aspect of your life.
2. Life is meant to be a meaningful, rewarding, joyous opportunity for all!

The Razzmatazz and Sexiness of Thoughtful Sophistication

Is your current level of thoughtful sophistication enhancing the quality of your experiences or improving upon the results you generate? If not, it is time to take a new approach. Thoughtful sophistication (self-awareness) is a competitive advantage to have in life and love because, with it, we display leadership and confidence, make better choices, take stronger actions, have more rewarding results, and showcase a sexy personality. Thoughtfully sophisticated or not, your personality, aka, charisma, magnetism, charm, powers of attraction, and personal values influence your choices, decisions, and life daily, whether or not you are aware of the impact of these silent influencers. Why not be more of an active participant in your unfolding? Understand the silent influencers shaping your life: your personality, your values, and your visions for happiness. Learn more about your unique charm and understand your hardwiring. Once you do, you are poised to then leverage your personality for a more satisfying and rewarding life experience as a thoughtfully sophisticated woman!

A thoughtfully sophisticated woman is confident because she knows her strengths, her weaknesses, and her blind spots. The self-aware woman is thoughtfully sophisticated and aware of her potential. She lives her life with more creatively and zest and opens herself up to the possibilities around her. Thoughtfully sophisticated women get more promotions, have more job satisfaction, are sexier, and have better personal and professional leadership skills. If you are willing to increase your self-understanding, you can "easily" become this woman and reap all the associated rewards. Any one of us can be thoughtfully sophisticated, it is an easy process. Start by answering these questions for self-understanding, know why/what/who/how/when/where you feel the happiest. Upon identifying the triggers that make you happy, make effort, to find more of those situations/opportunities/people. Do this consistently and you will feel happier, more often!

Researchers have concluded that only 10 to 15% of the population are thoughtfully sophisticated, (self-aware). In my opinion, this surprisingly low number is reflective of the general discomfort most of us have with questions, answers related to feelings. Except, unless we make the effort required to get comfortable with our feelings, we remain stuck exactly where we are, feeling exactly how we do. Therefore, let's get comfortable with just noticing our feelings. Eventually if we sincerely and consistently do this, we produce positive change. The hallmark of a thoughtfully sophisticated woman is she is continually progressing! Be that woman who takes her cues from within and confidently leads with the truth of her feelings which she has filtered with her situational awareness. It is her willingness to apply her self-awareness; direct her voice and express her needs that produce for her better results, and give her a unique competitive advantage… ***How is that NOT Sexy?!***

Knowing who you are means you're mindful of your personality, your motives, your strengths, your weaknesses, your passions, and your desires. These are the variables which create our realities; regardless of whether or not you are consciously aware of this fact. Feelings communicate our satisfaction level of the current realities. When you know who you are and why you are feeling what you are feeling, you have control over the current situation. You deserve to be confident and feel great. You can stop apologizing for feeling what you feel and wanting what you want. Be that woman who exudes sexiness just by embracing the truth of her uniqueness! "Hot bodies" eventually get warm, change shape and form, whereas a sexy personality endures! Your personality is a power of attraction, develop your personality more because the thoughtfully sophisticated woman understands and accepts who she is: If she doesn't like something about herself or her situation, she improves upon it. This is the kind of approach which exemplifies a sexy mindset! The thoughtfully sophisticated woman is cool, and has a sense of humor, she doesn't take herself too seriously—she knows who she is!

The Concepts

After nearly 20 years of successful experience as an accomplished Executive Life Coach, the three self-awareness concepts of personality, personal values, and a personal vision are what I've evidenced as most directly influencing personal satisfaction, success, and sexiness in life. Variables such as values, passions, aspirations, current environments, thoughts, feelings, behaviors, strengths, and weaknesses all merge to dictate our reality. Thoughtful sophistication enables you to 1). Know those variables, and 2). Better manage this inside-out process.

K.I.S.S. is full of stories of women who want 'more'. Some of the stories will resonate for you more deeply than others, in each story there is learning available.

I'll start by sharing a bit of my journey: I had been with my, then husband, for 13 years, with two children below the age of 4. I had married Jeff right out of University before I had any true understanding of myself. "On paper," Jeff was exactly what I most wanted, a good guy completely different from the family of men I grew up with. In the absence of thoughtful sophistication, I thought those were the right reasons to marry. However, unfortunately, at 35 I ended my marriage. It is important to me that my children, now adults, be self-aware and make all their choices with their thoughtful sophistication.

Regardless of who we are, until, and unless, we understand ourselves, we play small! And when we play small, we don't notice the multitude of choices and options that come with thoughtful sophistication. Without this kind of awareness, we end up causing avoidable damage. It doesn't have to be that way. Trial and error are not the only conduits for progress. It is possible to avoid making the same mistakes or having the same challenges countless women before you have had. You get to be more creative and battle new challenges! You will be reading about clients and participants personal and professional experiences and be introduced to a process you can learn and benefit from. Do the simple exercises, answer the questions that appeal to you, and, or sign up for your map forward and our 4-week online course, www.mapforward.org/success. Live your potential, sooner than later.

You have everything you need to live the life you truly want! Get Curious!

Personal Inventory

The best way to affirm, for yourself, that you have been blessed with everything you need is by doing a personal inventory. Consider getting yourself a dedicated journal to make notes in. The easiest, fastest, but an incomplete way to become a more thoughtfully sophisticated woman is by identifying for yourself which answer best represents your personality style:

1. What motivates you: results, or consensus?
2. Do you work best alone or do you prefer communicating and influencing others?
3. Do you have a sense of urgency, or do you prefer to plan, and be more methodical?

4. Do you love to "blue sky" and consider all the options/possibilities, or do you prefer exactness and specificity?

5. Do you notice you prefer to do things as you've always done, or do you take your cues from others?

6. Do you tend to process all incoming information via your heart (feelings), or via your head (logic)? And, lastly,

7. Do you like to do things as they've always been done, or do you naturally always think outside of the box and ask how things could be done differently or better?

Whatever your answers, they are perfect, because who you are, is who you are. Judge nothing and instead direct your energy towards ensuring you play to your strengths and account for your blind spots, which are the opposite of your strengths. A little further in the chapter, you will be able to assign the technical names for each of these personality traits.

With even just this loose acknowledgment that you have a processing style, you are positioned to make better more informed choices in favor of your style. When we choose in favor of our strengths we directly and positively impact outcomes! You are, and always will be, your most powerful tool and vehicle, for the success you seek. The more we play to our natural style, the better results we generate for ourselves! The more you understand your charisma/personality, the easier it is to shake off the past. Awareness offers perspective, enabling us to lovingly accept we do what we do based on how well and accurately we assessed the situation at the time. Perspective enables us to patiently shake off the negative feelings of past regrets as we shift our energy and attention to the present. Learn from the success or mistakes of past experiences, and make better choices, take better actions, and have new, better, different experiences. With self-understanding and thoughtful sophistication, it is so much easier to manage setbacks, visions, and aspirations that may arise.

Develop "know-how." Consistently apply the best of you, even the parts of you that others don't appreciate or have told you are useless.

Abundance is your destiny and everything about you is relevant! You are perfect. Your perfection is not dependent on family, upbringing, looks, or things "out there." Your "perfection" is a function of having been created in the likeness of God. Account for whom you are on the "inside," as a function of your nature (hardwiring) and your nurturing (upbringing). The nurture variables were the uncontrollables on the "outside": upbringing, bad breaks, job losses, and, or other people's agendas which have shaped our personality. These "out there" variables can leave us feeling voiceless and vulnerable. If you want to progress from where you are and how you are currently feeling, focus on your nature (values), it is our nature that others cherish, and it is your nature that will most directly get you to your Throne! You have the ability to refresh your eyes, increase your sophistication, and see only possibilities and opportunities.

The Lens of Science

There is a form of artificial intelligence (AI), that exists in the field of behavioral science, specifically referred to as a psychometric. These standardized tests are the same sort of criteria used to establish IQ. With this particular form of AI, personal information, the kind which leads to greater understanding, purpose, and better results, is available. The specific personality profile I have been working with for two decades, enables and increases awareness of an individual's potential. Clients receive a scientifically valid, reliable, and objective overview of their 7 most powerful personality traits. My sincere hope is that some of you, if not all of you, will sign up for the 4-week online course, www.mapforward.org/success, and access your profile. This technology has proven to be a game-changer for many, including me, and has the potential, to be the same for you!

This specific assessment, when understood, enables a unique profound understanding. Clients appreciate the ability to see a snapshot of their personality and its alignment with their career, in a graphical representation. The report, including the verbiage and the graphs, is a function of algorithms and fancy technology. The intention of this psychometric is to harness high performance, enhance self-understanding, enable decisive leadership, and build confidence! Your psychometric report will also help you accept who you are not: no more telling yourself you have to fake, try, or hope to be someone else. You have the opportunity to really see and understand what makes you unique, perfect, and Royal. It's time to embrace and celebrate the worthy, excellent, perfect woman you are!

The seven key traits Behavioral Scientist have identified as driving results are:

1. Assertiveness
2. Sociability
3. Pace
4. Detail Orientation
5. Behavioral Adaptability
6. Creativity
7. Emotiveness

These seven personality traits are listed in the same order as the processing style questions you identified for yourself in the first exercise.

What motivates you: results, or consensus? = **Assertiveness** is the trait.
If you are motivated by results, you are **assertive**.
If you are motivated by consensus/harmony, you are **accommodating**.
Both sets of behaviors are important and valuable.

Do you work best alone or do you prefer communicating & influencing others? = **Sociability** is the trait.
If you work best alone, the tendency may be more **task-focused**.
If you prefer communicating & influencing others, you are **relationship-oriented**.
Both sets of behaviors are important and valuable.

Do you have a sense of urgency, or do you prefer to plan, and be more methodical? = **Pace** is the trait.

Your pace either operates with **a sense of urgency or is methodical and process-oriented**.

Both sets of behaviors are important and valuable.

Do you love to "blue sky" and consider all the options/possibilities, or do you prefer exactness and specificity? = **Detail orientation** is the trait.

If you love to "blue sky" and resist exactness, you are a big picture thinker.

If you prefer exactness and specificity, you are **detail oriented**.

Both sets of behaviors are important and valuable.

Do you notice you prefer to do things as they've always been done, or do you tend to do as others want of you? = **Behavioral adaptability** is the trait.

If you prefer to do things as they've always been done, your behavior adaptability is somewhat limited; "what you see is what you get."

If your preference is to do as others want of you, you tend to play to the audience; "go along to get along."

How do you tend to process incoming information, via your heart (emotions), or your head (logic)? = **Emotiveness** is the trait.

Are you a **feeler or a thinker?**

Both sets of behaviors are important and valuable.

And, lastly,

Do you like to do things as they've always been done, or do you naturally think outside of the box at how things could be done differently or better? = *Creativity* is the trait.

If you are someone who likes to do things as they've always been done, creativity is not important to you.

If you are someone who naturally thinks outside of the box at how things could be, creativity is important to have active in your life. Both sets of behaviors are important and valuable.

These traits, regardless of how we feel about our natural processing style, are what dictate and influence, directly and indirectly, every aspect of our day-to-day life; everything from the results we generate in life to our compatibility with partners. We can adopt new behaviors/approaches, but we cannot change our hardwiring. The fact is though, the more you play to your natural strengths and design, the better and more sustainable all your results will be. Go with your flow! When you do, you will never, ever, make a wrong decision for yourself again, if you live your life informed by your personality and the key values you were uniquely assigned. When we make ourselves adopt behaviors outside of our natural operating style, we add unnecessary stress to our lives and create a bunch of other consequences that we are not easily able to respond to well in the moment. Don't judge your personality. Ultimately, it is your values that have the most powerful and influence over the quality of your experience and existence. Whereas personalities are a function of learned behavior and upbringing, our values just are. Still, there is huge value in first understanding your personality to know "how to" and "what to" maximize within your unique hardwiring. You have more than you realize available to you! Plus, in times of stress, we always revert to our familiar natural, learned styles. Therefore, if you recognize, and understand your unconscious tendencies/habits, the more likely you are to make better life-affirming choices! Science has established that people are predictable; you are predictable, I am predictable. Account for your predictability by making choices that support the truth of who you are: Set yourself up for success. Self-understanding makes us stronger.

Our 4-week online course, Self-Awareness for Success, is focused on ensuring you have and apply self-understanding to achieve better results and achieve the kind of success you crave! Participants of our program receive a detailed profile of their personality, relative to the 7 traits you've already been introduced to, and relative to each trait. Participants also receive a visual depiction of their alignment/compatibility, with their current job or area of focus. Then, for four weeks, and five times a week, for almost 20 hours, the focus is on ensuring you understand everything you want to understand in your report and as it relates to your transformation. At the end of the 4-weeks, you will receive a certificate of completion. The hours on the certificate qualify as unverified professional development. These pieces, along with me as your coach, empower, enable, and encourage you to achieve your desired transformation. You also receive exclusive access to our online communality and have regular direct contact with me. If you want, you can register for regular 1:1 coaching and video chats with me too, www.mapforward.org/success. Incidentally, the psychometric profile is a great, easy, efficient way to find true compatibility in a business or romantic partner. Behavior Adaptability makes it harder to establish if the kind of alignment that is needed for truly successful partnerships is present. For sustainable partnerships, individuals are looking together in the same direction, and not just looking at each other. It is easy to scoff at the notion of making effort and spending money to better understand yourself but get over that misguided perspective and recognize it as an investment opportunity which yields results you've not yet achieved! In many ways, our 4-week online course offers a much more tangible and fulfilling ROI, (Return on Investment) than a university degree. Having both a university degree and my personality profile with coaching, hands down, the knowledge, and personal insights from my personality, values, and vision have taken me further professionally and personally, than I ever imagined. The concrete relevant *life-enhancing* learnings are what have enabled me to excel as a businesswoman, entrepreneur, and mother.

Ask yourself if the path you are on is elevating your natural God-given potential. If not, why not, what is getting in the way? How and what could make your current choices and path more inspiring? This isn't about "needing" to do something different; it is about whether or not you "want" a different experience. On a scale of 1–10, how satisfied are you with your results and level of fulfillment?

In section 2 of *K.I.S.S.* we discuss the concept of personal values. In the course, we help you understand your personality profile, and identify your values. Both of these concepts are hugely important to your overall success. Like with any pursuit that stands to net us great returns, diligence and effort are required. You know the meaningful results you want, focus on those results, define Success, and Sexiness however you want! Be open to a proven safe process you can trust and reliably follow to help you. You deserve to be on the road less paved and living your values. Our values are our success triggers! Your success values have been patiently waiting for you to engage them, so you claim your Throne, change lives, and make the world a better place! All you are required to do is be curious about the infinite ways you can claim your Throne! However, allow me to be upfront with you though it could be a deal-breaker for some of you: You may have to be patient, more patient than you naturally are or want to be. Not a forever kind of patience, just the kind of patience that cannot be overly focused on immediate, tangible progress. I assure you, it will come, just not necessarily immediately. Although, it could. It's just that we are so accustomed to trusting our eyes, lack of tangible progress makes us self-doubt, give up, blame the strategy, or ourselves and abort. We don't like to be patient. If you can be patient, however, and follow this process, you will not be disappointed: abundance will seek you out. If values have never been a part of your unfolding, as is the case for many of us; that's ok. Learn now, why they are worthy of celebration and how you can use your personal values to be whatever you want to be. They are what give you your superhero powers! The unique defining values you have are to empower and enable you to flourish and make the world a better place! Our values are so powerful they can mitigate against any limits we perceive in our personalities and get us onto our paths of abundance. When we don't consciously and actively access and engage our values though, they can't do their job and guide us to our pot of gold. Unless we understand the powerful role of personal values, we may not ever really look within and know they are there to ensure our lives are meaningful, satisfying, and rich! However, with your personal values actively present you claim your Throne as the Queen you are, gracefully and effortlessly.

Meet Tanya

Meet Tanya, whose name, like the others you'll meet, has been changed

At first, Tanya, a millennial participant of MaP Forward didn't understand the power of her own personal values and feared accepting and embracing them. Her values were different from the values her loving parents had taught her and Tanya thought that embracing values different from mom/dad meant she was rejecting them. The values she had identified for herself, were different than what her parents wanted. They valued traditional proven societal models. Tanya valued Truth. Tanya was considering marrying a person who would be an acceptable match based on her upbringing and her parent's approval. However, she recognized the values that inspired her were not values he was very interested in. The compatibility of partners is dictated, in large part, by the presence of shared values. Tanya realized it would be in her best interest to step back and reframe how she was processing everything. She told him she needed more time to contemplate his proposal.

You will be introduced to many women like Tanya who confronted disconnects in their lives; personally, and professionally. It always boils down to choice, and each of us chooses between the two wills available:

permissive will (control) and perfect will (trust). Permissive will is about doing whatever we want, however, we want and whenever we want. Perfect will is about trusting in our truth; listening to our soul and being open to being guided by our values. Inevitably, our paths in life follow in the direction of the will we choose Control or Trust.

Meet Cindy

Cindy is a millennial client who found significant value in her profile. Cindy felt it was time for her to shake things up a little because she was bored, restless, and not feeling inspired by her own life. It wasn't a decision she made lightly, but she knew if you didn't enter a meaningful pattern interrupt, she risked always living variations of the only life and approach she knew.

Her initial strategy was to just keep switching jobs. She found the approach exhausting. Though it did temporarily alleviate some of her boredom; the whole process drained her. She had dreams but tended to dismiss them because when she would share them, she was usually told the dreams were too lofty and complicated for her to realize. Since Cindy didn't know otherwise, she figured those with whom she was consulting knew best and she didn't have what it would take.

Cindy's frustration grew, she was trying, but not seeing the progress she wanted. Finally, after repeated efforts and dismal results, she decided to take a step back and reconsider her approach. Cindy signed up for her map forward, received her personality report, and learned how to understand her potential. It informed her objectively, from a strength-based perspective and enabled her to consider herself in ways she hadn't.

Cindy trusted the information because she accepted the science behind the technology. The report of her profile, and the visual graphs of it, resonated with whom she knew herself to be, but it was differed from how others saw her. Interestingly, it didn't take her long to process the truths in her report and embrace the content in the program. It did, however, make her acknowledge that she had spent most of her life not living the fullness of her potential.

While her profile was undeniable for her and she had sensed much of what it stated about her abilities, motivators, and strengths, she had always dismissed her truths. She didn't know how to or if she could direct her potential; nobody else ever commented on it. Sadly, it is possible to ignore our potential and many do without realizing the implications of such a choice. Unfortunately, those who have chosen for the short-term, or took the easier path and let life pass them by, are not able to easily direct, comment, or speak to the subject of potential. Trust your feelings.

Values were the most challenging concept for Cindy to get her head around. She knew what she felt and wanted more of but didn't know those aspirations were legitimate pursuits. Cindy knew she wanted more excitement, and sensed she was creative, but creativity was never a big part of any jobs she applied for or an active part of her life. The lack of creativity in her jobs and life contributed to the almost constant state of boredom she felt and is why she would quit most of the jobs. When she began to approach the totality of her life more creatively, her feelings of helplessness dissipated and all of her results got better; things, in general, became more interesting for her!

Cindy knew she wasn't a huge people person and preferred to work alone, at her own pace but judged herself for not being more participative in-group settings and tried to fake it. This approach wasn't satisfying for her. When her profile helped her accept that she could be successful as the person she was, she began directing her strong affinity for creativity to finding more authentic behaviors that enabled her to celebrate her unique design and live her success triggers (values). In her past, she used approaches/strategies that worked for others without accounting for her own style and potential. She began to give *herself permission to use her creative mind and revisited some of the opportunities she had let go—because others told her "they weren't "realistic" opportunities for her."*

Tanya and Cindy, both allowed their profiles, and the formula, to positively impact their overall satisfaction, success, and sexiness! They confronted the truth of their "why," "what," "when" and "how" and chose to stop playing to other people's agendas, expectations, and desires for their own lives. Assign more meaning to your feelings, that is, restlessness... what might you be feeling restless for? Give yourself a chance to live the fullness of your potential, now. Say yes to the experience of living, but I only say that if you commit to doing it in Faith. Advance in your life while your energy, vision, and hope can all be harnessed for your greatest Joy!

You don't need a book or a course to tell you how you feel! This book and course are to:

1. Encourage you to embrace your feelings and then
2. Put your feelings to work for you within a context, formula, process that when followed, leads you to abundance.

Who you are matters!

Make your choices and decisions with thoughtful sophistication, awareness of who you are. All you are required to do to be more successful is to incorporate consistency. Upon understanding how you achieve your best results, ensure your choices complement the magnetism of your personality, values, and visions! For example, "if you have identified yourself as a consensus, harmony-oriented person, don't put that key piece of personal information in the drawer and choose jobs or people that are rigid or expect you to be forceful." Or if you have a sense of urgency, don't choose highly process-oriented jobs, such jobs will not set you up to shine and will bore you. Trust your feelings when you make choices. Make choices that motivate and inspire. It is not always easy to find inspiration, but if you at least know what to look for you increase the options available to you and have general ideas as to where you are likely to find more of what you seek. Take my professional experience for it, when we know what we can trust and rely on within ourselves, we naturally open up to all the possibilities and opportunities around us. We have more control over our current and future reality. It's not rocket science; it's a conscious process. When none of the options available to you inspire or motivate you, look within and remember you have the ability to create more options and by doing so; BAM, your life is more exciting and interesting! Broaden your job search, date more, sign up for the 4-week online course and learn how to set yourself up for success, satisfaction, and even more sexiness! Your Throne awaits you!

The individuals we consult with as Cindy did, have good intentions. The opportunities we share with select individuals though, may not be excellent opportunities from their vantage point and as such, the value of their input, at that exact moment is limited. Everyone has a unique vantage point informed by their unique personality and driving values. Consult with those who understand how you think or embrace the same values as you. When it comes to choices that impact only you and your results, only account for and allow for your vantage point to matter. Of course, be open to receiving guidance, but let yourself acknowledge that not all guidance and sources are equal. Accept the guidance that enables you to play to your strengths and honors your intelligent design! Your visions and values inform the Truth of your essence. Start making smarter, better, more aware choices that account for who you are, what you want, and what you are trying to achieve! Advance in life with thoughtful sophistication.

You have been created with everything you need to handle every opportunity, challenge, setback, loss, or disappointment life puts in front of you. There is nothing you can't do or overcome with awareness and focus. You are stronger than you realize. A map forward, using the profile of your excellent personality, a guided process, and me as your coach, is an easy, efficient way to ensure you get to where you are going, sooner and on your terms!

Abundance is your destiny. The world has a very specific need for you, now, do not tolerate any more delays: you are going to great places.

Receive Dr. Seuss's eloquent affirmation from his famous: Oh, the Places You'll Go! Children's book, published by Random House, New York:

"Today is your day. You're off to Great Places! You're off and away."

Chapter 2

The Power of Awareness—Exercises

Awareness, is a powerful concept. It is, also, a great starting point for thoughtful sophistication. The more "aware" you are of things like your personality, motivating values, energy, feelings, risk orientation, people, and possibilities both the ones you see, as well as the ones you only sense; the clearer your options for a more satisfying life become. As you create options for yourself, almost miraculously more options begin to present themselves. With increased options, you have more choices to choose amongst. As you learn to be more decisive, the accumulation of small and big decisions you make lead to transformation!

Owing to the multitude of choices we make every minute of every day, the more choices we make with an awareness of our God-given potential, the more we set ourselves up to thrive! Our satisfaction, success, and sexiness are and always will be a function of the choices we make, whether they are big or small. Each choice we make sets off a sequence of events that either empower us or disempower us; either we make our choices with intentional awareness or we do not. Those are the only two options. For example, if you know you value consensus and harmony, but choose to pursue leadership roles or date aggressive men; your integrity and self-respect may be compromised, unnecessary stress may get generated, and results suffer. If leadership is an aspiration, great, nail the behaviors associated with leadership before you throw your hat into the ring otherwise, it will be unnecessarily stressful. If you are okay with these odds, advance, or wait till the odds are more in your favor. In the same way, if you value process, but exist in a role where you are required to deliver speedy results, not afforded the time to deliver the quality and results important to you, your performance, results, and confidence will be compromised.

The more you understand the behaviors associated with your personality traits, the easier it is to "win" on the right paths, with the "right" partners. You don't need to be a different person or get more education, get more education because you want to learn more—not because someone tells you or you think that without it you won't succeed.

You are great, and that was established years ago, for you. Who you are now, is more or less who you will always be. The sooner in life you understand the person you are, the less time you waste or lose trying to be someone you are not. By focusing and directing your energy to who you are, inevitably you live a more satisfying and productive life journey! I am absolutely sure that your design is intelligent and perfect because God designed you and your essence. Make more choices with this awareness. You have everything you need to succeed! God has an ownership stake in your unfolding. It is He, who handpicked your defining values for you. Therefore, tap into His assistance. Ask for His help and understanding; ask for whatever you want! Ask Him from wherever you are, and whenever you want to. He's cool, chill, the specifics aren't as important to

Him, He just wants your focus and willingness to ask for His help, i.e., "Hey God, I need your help." If you want His help in specific ways, tell Him. Then, wait for it. I assure you; it will come.

> *"Ask and it will be given to you; seek and you will find; knock and the door will be opened to you." Matthew 7:7 (NIV)*

Increase Your Awareness

Just as "Location, location, location" is the mantra of real estate agents, so "Awareness, awareness, awareness" is the mantra of personal and professional development coaches. The starting point of all change is awareness, therefore, increase your awareness. As we increase awareness of our daily lives we produce change, though all we are doing is "noticing" more. Get into the habit of noticing everything: people, opportunities, thoughts, the kinds of risks you take each day, how many new people you interacted with, notice the times when you were bold, notice the times held back, notice how many people you showed love to today. Notice who and what bores you. Notice who and what you really enjoy. Notice how many times you did, and, how many times you did not, give deserving compliments...notice EVERYTHING; including what you tolerate that drives you bonkers or what you dismiss, because you don't know how to address the situation. This simple exercise will open your eyes to all the opportunities in front of you to improve your situation, now. We may choose to not address each and every issue and instead develop a decision-making process to determine when we will address issues and when we won't. Notice the personal or professional cost to you when you take a pass on your progress. You are worthy of the life you want and unless you are willing to acknowledge your life as it is, it's hard to improve upon your life experience and realize what could be.

Your Throne is awaiting you; you can do this!

The more we notice, the more intentional we are, it just plays out that way. Hence why the more you notice, the more you make changes. Journal, what you notice. Jot down what matters to you; what feelings you want more of. Journal your satisfaction or level of happiness: are you happy, are you somewhat happy? Notice who and what influences your happiness. Try to notice the specific things, people, areas of your life that drain your energy; when and where you may be selling out on yourself; when and where in your life you know you hold back. Notice and celebrate situations, people, or things that make you feel unstoppable. Notice, and then avoid, as you can, the situations, people, and feelings that do not enable or empower you. Conscious awareness is required to make changes, and have better results, success, and sexiness. Notice everything and watch how quite naturally your observations influence your actions when you let them. No different than when you notice rain coming inside an open window... chances are, without much thought, you'd move to close the window.

The thoughtfully sophisticated woman will apply that same obvious rationale to her own life. For example, when you notice something is out of whack, not as you want for it to be, you'll quite naturally take action to make it better, i.e., Close the window.

You already have everything you need to realize your ideal life, now, let's organize your excellence. All it takes to organize your excellence is to understand it. It's easier to believe in your excellence when you understand your personality/charisma/magnetism/charm and power of attraction. Your personality is your excellence, understand it so you can organize it. Use your self-understanding to **identify the situations that elevate you and make you feel great**. Now, organize your excellence by actively finding more opportunities to be elevated. Notice the themes that emerge in the choices you make, by that I mean notice what types of things, people, experiences, and opportunities you consistently choose in favor of. Use your awareness to make better choices, choices which support your growth and desired transformation. Know what to look for by using your personality style. Identify the jobs, people, opportunities, or situations where your unique personality is appreciated and needed. Your uniqueness is wanted and needed in the world and you can very easily have a more satisfying life just by letting everyone and anyone know what you have to offer. You don't have to rush the process or force the paths.... Be encouraged by Dr. Seuss, and remember,

"...you may not find any you'll want to go down. In that case, of course, you'll head straight out of town. It's opener there in the wide-open air...and when things start to happen, don't worry. Don't stew. Just go right along. You'll start happening too." —Dr. Seuss, *Oh, the Places You'll Go!*

Trust that your energy will make manifest, your excellence

Focus on what you can influence and keep increasing your thoughtful sophistication. Embrace your thoughtful sophistication. Believe in your potential for success and sexiness! Follow the process in this book, sign up for the companion 4-week online course, www.mapforward.org/success, and engage with me and others, in our online community. The goal of the course is to help you understand the fullness of your potential and achieve transformation! Maybe for the first time in your life, you will consider your potential: what are you good at, how do you want to direct your attention, what types of results are you willing to work for, what motivates you? The effort required to claim your Throne as the Queen you are is completely within your realm of possibility, and there is a process you can follow and trust.

While challenges, setbacks, losses, and/or disappointments occur, slow us down and may even sabotage our efforts, those situations are not stronger than who you have been designed to be. Develop your resilience by identifying and understanding the breadth and depth of your strengths and account for your blind spots. You have more options than you realize, develop your map forward, and see them clearly. Live as the sexy suave thoughtfully sophisticated Queen you have been designed to be. You are too good to settle for less than the best and if it feels like a scary proposition, take heart because you are not alone to claim Your Throne:

> *"The Lord is the one who goes ahead of you; He will be with you. He will not fail you or forsake you. Do not fear or be dismayed." Deuteronomy 31:8 (NASB).*

As you increase your awareness and thoughtful sophistication, you will naturally shift from being externally focused to being internally focused. It will become clearer to you how, where, when, and why you are more successful and sexier in some places than others. The sooner you begin to think this way, and set yourself up to succeed, the sooner you will arrive.

Defining Moments and Purpose

Our life experiences, results, success, and purpose are influenced and determined by our personalities and values.

Read that again. Do you understand what that means?

You can have better more direct control over your outcomes!

YOU can generate more of the experiences you want!

You can navigate through the less than ideal experiences you face and move to ensure you have fewer of them! How? By applying your awareness for mostly, only, life-affirming choices. Life-affirming choices are the ones that energize you AND move your forward. Identify how, when, what, and who, energizes you, and give thought as to where you want to get to in your life. Of course, our desired destinations may change, all that matters is you start to take better and more control over your life as the Captain of your ship!

Below are the questions my clients have found directional. Consider the questions from the perspective of your life now and jot the answers down in your journal. I suggest you give yourself time to digest your responses before you move on to the next question. Reflect upon your responses.

In your journal, identify three key moments, when you **achieved results that made you feel great**. What feelings did you feel, what did you love about the results you achieved?

Next, identify three **noteworthy challenges you've dealt with in your life.**

In both scenarios, results, and challenges, what feelings do you remember feeling?

What enabled you to realize the results you did? It may have been the same feelings, and actions for both questions, and maybe not. There is no wrong answer. An example of an answer could be, you were focused on a specific result, or it could be a feeling of determination, frustration, etc.

Take note of the situations/moments that have historically **got you into action** or **feeling motivated** or **inspired**. In your journal, think back to a **demotivating job, or a relationship with an unworthy suitor, and reflect on how you got yourself into those situations**. Take note of **what made you chose that job or that suitor. What did that choice do for you, and what did that choice cost you**?

In each of these moments, something important related to your purpose and personal values was reinforced for you; examine those moments/situations more closely. Sometimes our purpose hits us obviously, and other times we are required to dig for it. The exercises offered are to provide you with a framework by which you can access your thought process.

These are the types of questions that help us find themes, specific feelings (values), strengths, and responses that have moved us in the past and shaped our character. Notice any other questions that come up for you. This kind of personal information, when reflected upon, helps us establish a purpose for our lives. If nothing comes up for you now though, that's okay.

It's boring and safe to only and always approach life based on what we know and understand. When we stick to only what is in front of us, or what is easiest; we don't allow for surprises that may delight us, where's the fun, excitement or growth, in that! In section 2, on Focus, we discuss Vision, more. Visions are expansive, new, unfamiliar, exciting, meaningful, and fun! Therefore, to not let yourself have a compelling, motivating, inspiring, meaningful vision of what could be, is to live without hope. Without the hope of "more," whether that is for more results, more growth, or a more satisfying and fulfilling approach to our lives, we risk only ever living a continuous, never-ending loop of the same types of experiences, jobs, and relationships…, such approaches do not advance the aspiring Queen who is ready to claim her Throne!

The more you understand the patterns in your life vis a vis your jobs, relationships, and choices, the more you can control, direct, improve, or make changes in your life! Learn how to trust your energy for decision making. Trust that it is always better to play the long game and let your energy guide your choices. Only choose that which energizes you. Don't take a job or date a person that bores you, better options are en route. At the same time, within the choices you make, whether that is for a course of study, job, or partner, there may be moments of drain and dread, just be sure you are or can sincerely be energized by at least a few solid aspects of that which you choose. When we consistently make our choices thinking only of the short term; the paycheque, or ease, or convenience, or practicality, or companionship, we risk losing the inspiration needed for excellence. Without inspiration and hope, we lower the likelihood of ever realizing our potential. When we forsake our mojo, even if "just for the short term," we risk becoming complacent. The willingness to tolerate complacency is a slippery slope which too easily results in lost mojo! Your mojo is worth defending AND, you are worthy of a Throne!

In your journal, decide now: **Is your best outcome a life of adventure, a life full of meaningful purpose, or a day-to-day existence?** Whatever lifestyle you aspire for, ensure your choices lead you in that direction. The more empowering your choices, the sooner you'll claim your Throne, as the Queen of you!

In your journal, **take note of what others appreciate about you. And decide, how much you cherish those same abilities, about yourself?** For example, Gurpreet had the gift of gab and was naturally effective at influencing people to take action. Her peers and siblings would often encourage her to find sales jobs where she could use her abilities and make lots of money. Gurpreet admitted that while she loved what money could do for her, money it of itself, was not a huge motivator for her, and the thought of using her ability to influence, only to make lots of money held no appeal for her.

Telling you about Gurpreet because while others appreciated this ability in her, it did not resonate for her as a strategic motivating opportunity. She was open to using her powers of persuasion, but only if she felt it was for a worthwhile pursuit. These simple exercises are to help you make guided observations and consider your "purpose opportunities." What you write in your journal is for your eyes only.

Identifying Purpose

If you do not know where you are going, every road will take you there — Henry Kissinger. There is purpose hidden within each one of us; the key is to discover meaningful, purposeful opportunities, **opportunities that we sincerely care about.** As it's already been stated, to live your purpose, understand the nuances and excellence within your personality, values, and vision. There are many purpose opportunities for each of us. **The one, primary, true purpose we each have though, is to become who we were created to be.** From this informed position, what you choose is secondary, because, you will be successful at whatever you do. Many do not like the truth of this simplicity. They think it has to be a deeply complicated process and seem to tell themselves they must spend years looking for "their purpose." Use the fullness of your personality and values towards whatever vision of purpose you choose! **Be the person you have been designed to be and you will find your purpose: to excel and manifest a better world, for all!**

Maybe, this book is in your hands because you are ready to identify and name a vision of purpose that helps you to self-actualize. And if so, congratulations! You are not amongst the meek and timid souls who tolerate mediocrity; avoiding both victory and defeat. You are bold, brave, and courageous because you are ready for "more!" More, for yourself and from yourself! Awareness-raising is a fun easy exercise, but it is passive. To take new actions, and make bolder choices informed by your awareness is powerful! Play to win, move in the direction of your potential, keep your eyes focused on your Throne. It is only a matter of time before you live the life that you envision for yourself.

If past disappointments, challenges, and setbacks are holding you back and preventing you from moving forward, consider reframing the "yuck." Those disappointments, challenges, and setbacks were not in vain. They deepened the depth of your foundation. Imagine yourself a skyscraper. The higher skyscrapers are designed to go, the deeper must be the foundation that supports them. In the same way, it is your depth, that now enables you to go higher than you've been. Reframe the disappointments, pains, and difficulties you've had to overcome and understand they were to help you prepare you for the height of your potential, give you a glimpse of just how high you are destined to go.

The goal is transformation. Transformation, from the small, cute caterpillar, into the powerful, beautiful, brilliant, purpose-driven woman, butterfly, you are! In your journal, muse about what that could look like for you, **what could your best life be?** Will you define your best life by promotions and salary, or will you define your best life by becoming an entrepreneur, your own boss, or being paid well enough as an employee, or would you measure your best life by how you feel about yourself and the life you are living? Only you know what truly matters to you, and if you are willing to live for whatever vision you have, I assure you, it will be yours!

The #MeToo movement is a reminder to us as women that we are to defend our visions and paths forward. Though they may try, no one has the right to deny us, block us, hold us back, or change the paths we have chosen, or the desires in our heart. The moment, and the movement, favor our ascension. Therefore, turn the frown upside down. Focus on deepening your sense of self. The deeper your foundation the more empowered you are and the easier it is to pivot, and redirect when and if, you are being held back.

Your Inner Goddess

As a result, the moment and the movement, need us women to encourage each other to let our inner goddess out! Focus on what your vision for life, could be. Remember, you can call me. (disclaimer, it may take a few days before we end up connecting, but it will happen!). In the interim, continue increasing your awareness and allow the visions to grow in your mind. The clearer your vision is in your mind's eye, the easier it is for your inner goddess to direct you towards your desired results. Give no thought to what you don't know or don't have. Let yourself be excited about your plans, organize your potential, and test the waters, take some risks, have new discussions with new people. Saying yes to life, within reason, enables life to bring to you that which you desire and seek. Focus on the controllable. Develop focused clarity of what you want. Await the guidance you need, it will come: Wait for it!

> *"And whatever you ask in prayer, you will receive, if you have faith." Matthew 21:22 (ESV)*

Stand firm and claim your birthright, it is more than possible; it is your destiny. You can be assured it is your destiny because your unique personality, personal values, and vision, desires, and abilities, none of which you asked for, are uniquely yours. Everything you have, in some way or another, has been intentionally and strategically assigned to you! You are a product of an intelligent design and have a God-appointed destiny. While you may not subscribe to the Jesus message, the Truth still is: None of us asked to have what we had or have: upbringing, personality, intellect, looks, or values we do, and yet, these are the exact, specific, unique variables that establish and direct our success. No accidents, no coincidences. He is an all-knowing amazing God who works in mysterious ways. You are more than you currently realize: Wake up what may be lying dormant inside of you. You will be aided, guided, and restored if you accept, believe, and trust, that you are not alone on this journey. You shall be guided to your Throne.

> *"I will go before you and make the rough places smooth; I will shatter the doors of bronze and cut through their iron bars." Isaiah 45:2.*

Violations against your goddess; physical, mental, or emotional may have been morally and ethically wrong, and that is on them, the perpetrators. Take comfort in remembering your inner goddess is bigger than any setbacks. While you may not know, she knows that the self-doubt your setbacks may have caused is misplaced. Believe in your thoughtful sophistication. Focus on designing your path forward.

Shake off whatever you need to, focus only on the reality you crave.

Meet Laura

Laura had always wanted a map forward she could trust. She read self-help books, set goals for herself, and wanted a better life than she had growing up. Her mom had been mistreated by her dad and was left pennilessly unable to help herself. Laura's mom never seemed happy because she was living hand to mouth. Laura felt helpless that she couldn't do anything for her mom. Her only controllable was to ensure that she never found herself in the same situation. Laura knew that if she empowered herself in some way, she would also be helping her mom. Before she came to MaP Forward Inc., she went down too many blind alleys and said she was making too many bad choices. She couldn't figure out why her efforts were not working out better for her. The problem seemed to be that she was following models she had heard about, without actually modifying them to fit with her personality, values, and style. Laura didn't have much support in her life and told herself it was smartest to use the same approach others were succeeding with. She didn't know how else she could move forward. Laura's desires were right for her, she just had her ladders on the wrong walls. Her lack of thoughtful sophistication left her feeling like her only option was to do as others did. She felt alone. When you feel alone, please know, you are not. None of us are.

> *"Be strong. Be brave. Be fearless. You are never alone." Joshua 1:9 (LEB)*

Our system helped her to feel more like a victor in her own life. She moved to leverage more of her potential, and by doing so, was in a better position to help her mom do the same.

Chapter 3

In Choice—Exercises

G ood or Great?

"Good" is the unspoken standard. The collective seems to favor the status quo of "good"; regardless of how satisfying it is. Understandably, for many, "good" represents what they tell themselves they most want to feel—comfortable, safe, and secure. Except, life offers so much more than just comfort, safety, and security! To tap into the fullness of life's offerings, we are required to go beyond good to great, and we do this by vigilantly defending our visions. Vigilantly, we are required to resist the ever-present temptation to compromise, lower our standards, limit our potential, or be lulled complacent by good! Commit to your own greatness and by doing so, give your life more meaning and purpose. Take the inside-out approach and focus on being great. **Decide, if you are willing to choose. What's it going to be for you: Good or Great?**

What is good for others, may not be good enough for you. It is all relative. We are each a product of our hardwiring. You don't have to be satisfied with good, just because it is good—but you can be. You can just as naturally want "more." You can want greatness from yourself and in your life. From experience, professionally and personally, I assure you, in the actual, there are no personal limits. **We never reach our limits; we only think we do.** You are the Queen of You: Go claim your Throne.

Challenge More

Thoughtfully sophisticated women ask questions when they lack clarity. They challenge what they don't agree with, and they keep asking more questions until they understand. Give blind faith only to God. None of us, "have to" accept the way things are or do things we don't agree with, understand, or want. We are in choice every minute of every day. We may choose to challenge more of the mental models we're shaping our life around or we might not. It's less about what we choose and more about what we are trying to achieve. Keep your focus on what you are trying to achieve and choose the paths and people that reflect your essence and vision. Besides, most of our mental models are staid—the world needs more creative and innovative visions.

Your Reference Points and Risk-Taking

It's likely that school, activities, or others, left you with reference points that you may not be aware of, or even agree with—and yet still unconsciously, not only hold do you hold on to them, you probably live them out. The problem is whenever we unconsciously do anything, we become stuck without even knowing why, or how we got there! I highlight awareness-raising because without awareness it is hard to be fully present, most individuals do not even realize they are on mental cruise control. As you keep increasing your "awareness" however, you become very adept at problem-solving, and playing the long game, having perspective, achieving goals creatively; you are in control and in motion.

Often, our elders, parents, church, and school taught reference points that may not have been effectual or happiness producing. Yet, oddly enough, these same flawed mental models keep being handed down, with little thoughtful sophistication, the blind lead the blind. It's no one's fault that tradition influences so many of our big life decisions. We have the opportunity and responsibility, now, however, to lead with a more thoughtful sophistication and ask ourselves how we feel about those traditions. When we choose to challenge the traditions we've grown up with, we risk losing the blueprint that existed for our life. Tradition is safe, it helps us to manage our expectations, just as it effectively stifles change, however, the thought of not having a blueprint to follow could feel risky. However, you can do it! Risk-taking is an inherent part of all progress. It is a value and ability that is available to all of us! The risk is, what if, what if "it" doesn't work out? But what if, it did work out? What would you stand to gain?

With thoughtful sophistication, your relationship with "risk" can be a completely different proposition. Now, you can reframe "risk." If you actually stepped back and examined your relationship with risk a little more closely, chances are the aversion to risk is related to your upbringing. If a parent or someone close to us took risks that didn't play out well, we grow up associating risk with negative outcomes. With awareness, we can identify the origins of our limiting beliefs and reframe whatever we need to. If your experience with risk-taking has made you aversive to taking risks head-on, okay. Focus on what your personality is great at and look for the motivating values which can move you forward. Risk can be intimidating to accept, reframe it however you need until you develop this ability more. It is entirely respectable to approach and embrace risk, with caution. Identify the pieces of information you "need" to take the leap of "what if," faith. Any smart risk-taker does a certain degree of due diligence before they risk, some have just developed the ability to do it more naturally. When you are satisfied with your level of due diligence and okay with the worst-case scenario: Trust. At worst, being the creative, resourceful, and whole Queen, you are, there is a 50–50% chance of success. If you want better odds than that, determine what more information you need, and get it. You've got this.

Risk-taking is an ability that we are well served to develop! We live in a world where there is little to no reward without risk. If you want progress, success, and sexiness, develop your risk tolerance and risk orientation because risk you must. Unless we take risks to move forward, we will stagnate and then regress. Risk-taking is really about a willingness to lose. What are you holding on to that can't be replaced with something better? You are in control of your perspective and can reframe your perspective however you want and need to. It's only about your perspective, it's not about facts or absolute truths. Play the long game and focus on your personality, values, and vision of success. Minimize how risky something feels by making all your decisions informed and steeped in awareness of the truth of your potential, your values, and the worst-case scenario. Always remember: You have been hardwired to succeed. If you have a vision or desire for something that requires you to reach further than you've ever done-easy peasy, no sweat, you've got this—because if you didn't, the vision, desire, or hope would not persist! Of course, it is still possible that,

"...you will come to a place where the streets are not marked. Some windows are lighted. But mostly they're darked... Do you dare to stay out? Do you dare to go in? How much can you lose? How much can you win?" —Dr. Seuss, *Oh, the Places You'll Go!*

The point is, you can always do a re-do and in the interim use the time to acquire and develop a deeper sense of self, deepen your faith.

Acquire values like courage, and perspective, if you don't already have them. Each and every value that ever existed or ever could is available to you to get you to your Throne. Values that you don't naturally have, or relate easily too, can be acquired and developed! You are destined to succeed. Determine what you are willing to lose/risk for in exchange for your Throne. Such decisions are the moments of truth, which shape our character. Actively shape your character into that of a Queen: Choose boldly.

Add *"why not,"* to your self-talk. The biggest risk you can take in your life is to follow prescribed external models, reference points, and status quo's, without having ever truly examined them! When we follow, mostly or always, models that fail to account for our unique personality, values, and visions, we risk being stuck with identities and realities, that are a function of what others in society deem respectable. Such an approach will deny you, your Throne.

You're destined to be the person you were designed to be, get more actively involved in your own unfolding! YOU must chart your own journey. If, that feels too risky, call me so we can reframe your perspective, together. I care and want you to feel supported. Get more curious about what awaits you in your life; sign up for our 4-week course, "Self-Awareness for Success," www.mapforward.org/success! Trust your heart.

> *"The heart of man plans his way, but the LORD establishes his steps." Proverbs 16:9 (ESV)*

Focus on your potential, not your upbringing and reference points

Jessica, another client, seemingly had it made. She inherited her role and her company does very well. She is respected in her industry and makes lots of money. With her kids out of the nest, Jessica had more time on her hands and realized that despite her impressive life, she wasn't too sure of her identity. Her marriage was over, Jessica had health issues. She, herself, never really chose her job... The changes in her life were unsettling for her and affected her focus, effectiveness, and even the quality of her experiences. It was very uncomfortable for her, and so, courageously, she decided to search for her Truth. Many things came up for Jessica in her awareness-raising, including her history of surrounding herself with people who weren't as ambitious or thoughtfully sophisticated. She realized that she had been uninspired by her life for too long. She wanted help to grow and stretch.

I share Jessica's example to hopefully spare you from the same 20-20 hindsight...finally, after 20 years of sucking it up, she recognized that her life had been engineered to reflect what others wanted for her. Her reference models taught her to suck it up and just do what needed to be done. She did as she was taught, but that also included an eighteen-year incompatible marriage. Jessica wanted to blue sky and imagine what her life could look like, now, leading with her values and intuition rather than her reference points. She is finally willing, ready, and able to consider her options. While Jessica wished she had done it before her life got so entangled, she's not sure what choices she would have made differently. At least now, she is making informed decisions; better late than never.

In fairness to Jessica, and to all of us who chose our life path this way, it is not obvious or easy to know how else to "do it."

Blind Spots

Personality, in the broadest sense, is the psychological system that organizes our motives, emotions, awareness, intelligence, expression, actions, and self-control. *K.I.S.S. (Keep It Simple & Sexy); The Career Guide for Women Unwilling to Compromise*, offers you a comprehensive pathway to help you understand the brilliant complexity of you, including your strengths, and blind spots. Blind spots are generally the flip side of our strengths.

For example, Brenda has a natural sense of urgency, it is a key driver and motivator for her, which serves her very well in her marketing role. Brenda only ever focused on her flashy panache for doing things, which, therefore, became her blind spot. She was overly attached to her style and insisted on doing everything with passion, flair, and impatience. Her unsophisticated approach caused herself avoidable problems and she failed to account for the needs of others. She was too willing to sacrifice "quality" for "speed," as she deemed necessary. She gave no thought to methodology because it slowed her down, but as a result, her deliverables were not as thorough or as informed as they could have been. Brenda, in many ways, was true to her personality, her motivators, and her values but by doing so, she left herself vulnerable to her blind spots, including her low behavior adaptability. She got canned.

Failure to account for our blind spots can cause us significant setbacks. Sometimes, when we don't know how else to handle things, we tend to rely on our default, go-to style, regardless of its effectiveness or appropriateness for the situation at hand. With thoughtful sophistication, it is easier to step back, troubleshoot, and see different, new options and possibilities. It really is this simple!

Many of us are frustrated by efforts that didn't play out as we had hoped, been promised, or expected: You are not alone if that has been your experience. There are many unique challenges women face, and the types of issues the #MeToo movement has highlighted presents a unique opportunity for us. This movement, like other historical movements, serves as a catalytic opportunity for us women to re-evaluate our approach, identify our purpose, and better leverage all the potential that has been lying dormant within us.

If you have had opportunities denied you, felt held back, or maybe you didn't get a fair start on your path for abundance, take heart, not all has been lost, your best days are still ahead of you! It is our time, as women, to realize more of our greatness and direct it to the creation of new and better opportunities and possibilities for our lives. After almost two decades as a high-performance executive life coach, I have learned the simple and powerful truth, success comes through self-awareness. Regardless of our job title—President, CEO, employee, manager, mom, or student; real success requires thoughtful sophistication.

"You have brains in your head, you have feet in your shoes, you can steer yourself any direction you choose. You're on your own. And you know what you know. And YOU are the guy who'll decide where to go." —Dr. Seuss, *Oh, the Places You'll Go!*

Chapter 4
The #MeToo Era

K.I.S.S. is a guide to success, as such, I am dedicating this chapter to the #MeToo Era, for women already existing, or entering into the workforce. The #MeToo movement has shown it doesn't discriminate, and stories from women of all ages, nationalities, and social and economic backgrounds, have emerged. The challenges, women face as it relates to this issue will be with us for as long as women are women, and men are men. This truth is a function of many things, mostly the unevolved and undisciplined animal instincts of some men. Accordingly, forewarned is forearmed. Now, there is an opportunity to hold governments, corporations, and employers around the world accountable—but you can only do that if you recognize you are being played for a fool. The #MeToo Movement has been called a watershed moment in the advancement of gender equality, giving a powerful platform for women to make public the impact of the damages sexual harassment has across society. Gender equality is the opportunity, and the #MeToo movement is the rallying call and invitation for all women, to come out stronger and more definitively than we may have in the past. She, who understands herself, "wins" because she, who understands herself, manages her controllables.

Women have their gender used against them, often enough. Men disempower women this way often, subtly or otherwise. It isn't only in Hollywood; it's in Corporations all over the world and in every size of business/industry/environment where men hold the balance of power. Careers have been diminished by not going along with the self-serving strategy of perpetrators. Though we cannot control men's agendas for us. We can, however, lead with more awareness of how these predators operate and develop strategies that minimize the damage. Take for example, in cases of "Grooming." Predators target newer, younger women in places of employment. The unsuspecting, hopeful ambitious woman is offered assistance, support, and attention. The predators' intention is to develop rapport, break down existing barriers, formalities, and resistance. As the friendly professional relationship evolves victims are not suspicious, see no abuse of power. It works against women because finally when the advances are made, she believes she has been complicit, blames herself, doesn't complain/report, and may go along with the conduct. The perpetrator's strategy worked. Though it's ridiculous that women need to be bothered with such things, it's still very wise, in uncontrollable situations like this to focus on attitude and self-empowerment. The point is this:

"Whoever sows sparingly will also reap sparingly, and whoever sows bountifully will also reap bountifully." 2 Corinthians 9:6 ESV

Here's my #Metoo story, it's not a sensational one, I didn't get grouped or anything. Nope, mine was "just" creepy calculated and ultimately, career devastating: remember it and learn from it, mostly avoid your own #MeToo story. It is easy for powerful men to play unsuspecting women for fools. It's long; sit back, enjoy a warm beverage and I'll share.

Part 1

In my mid-30's, I was a self-employed, single mom, professionally certified Executive Life Coach, and had already been blessed with professional success. I also secured for myself, a fabulous opportunity with, as the media names them, one of the most powerful multinationals in the world.

I worked with five of their senior executives for several years, and this multinational was by no doubt, the highest-profile and lucrative client I had. They would fly me to the other side of the country, bi-weekly and overnight, and I would meet with each of them Friday morning and fly home Friday afternoon. Each of my client's mandates for our work together was met.

The most exhilarating mandate I received came from the Chief Operating Officer. He asked me to "ensure he get chosen to be the next CEO for the company, over his rivals." I delivered. The COO ended up being the biggest beneficiary of the professional relationship between our two companies. My client was chosen to be the new CEO, and even thanked me! **He went from a salary of $500, 000/ year to a salary of over 12 million dollars/year, not including stock options!!** *His company, its shareholders, and he earned huge profits during his tenure. He was often voted as the Best CEO in Canada! For me, this was a hugely positive career-defining moment....*

My client, the new President, and CEO, promised me more opportunities, and said I could work within their 7 local companies, and no longer have to fly to head office and be away from my young kids. Contingent on my ongoing effectiveness, he offered me the opportunity to resume travel and have more global opportunities, later.

When I asked him "how" to advance these tremendous professional opportunities locally, he told me to leave it with him and "trust him" to re-engage me. That seemed reasonable. Both the CEO and No. 2 in the company had been amongst my satisfied clients, and I trusted they would follow through. It also meant, however, that he alone would decide when and where to engage me in his company.

The CEO initiated several dinner meetings with me each year when he was local, to advance this discussion. It was encouraging, I was excited and ready to be re-engaged. I came to each dinner meeting expectantly, notebook clearly in hand, and prepared to take down names to get started. When I would ask direct and specific questions about a specific local leader, he would always respond with variations of the usual response, "not yet, trust me, I'm looking for the right opportunities/clients for you. Just keep your hat in the ring, let's continue our meetings, and I will let you know."

I was happy to "trust him" and still professionally support him during our dinners, though unpaid. Why not? He had publicly stated, "I was the reason he was in his role." Of course, he was the reason, but for him to give such public credit to a service provider... I remember sitting in the audience, amazed at what I was hearing him state! He knew I was self-employed, that my kids were little, and unlike him, I was still relatively early in my career. He also knew that the coaching space is saturated and understood the more work I could get with them, the more assured my professional success and access to other multinational corporations. Plus, he had both contacts and influence. So, I did as he advised and just kept meeting with him for dinner and being told to "trust me." This situation was the pattern for several years but with never any new business opportunities. I was perplexed and bewildered. He consistently kept telling me to trust him though. I believed him because he had no reason to lie or deceive me. For any business, salesperson, or entrepreneur, recurring clients are the lifeline of ongoing professional credibility. In my prospecting for new clients, I would name the globally well-known client and reference my success with/for them, and that did advance me.

Eventually though, as the years passed, the high-profile companies or CEO's I would try to sell my professional coaching services to, knew of the results I had generated for this company and others, plus, Mr. CEO's publicly stated accolades were amongst the testimonials in my marketing materials. Naturally, they asked about my ongoing work with the multinational, within any of the seven local offices. In the absence of any ongoing professional work with this multinational, the only honest answer I could give was that the CEO and I were meeting regularly and discussing this. To me, that was proof of the company's intent to re-engage me. I tried over the years to work through my other client, the VP of Human Resources, asking him if I could take it upon myself to solicit more business directly at the local offices, as I understood that my CEO client had other priorities. It seemed; the VP of HR would first confer with the CEO. Eventually, he would respond to my requests saying "no, other coaches were being used."

Something was off. His words were different from what Mr. CEO, was telling me. It never made sense to me that this multinational with so many local offices, leaders, women, and visible minorities, had NO opportunities for me, despite my impressive and successful track record with them. But, Mr. CEO, years after our work together, and at the same frequency was still requesting dinners meetings with me, promising me ongoing work and telling me to "trust him"; and after all, he had made such a public declaration of my effectiveness. It was in my best interest to "keep trusting him," and to keep meeting with him since that is what he told me it would take. I continued to answer the questions of prospective clients, with the only assurance I had, he was meeting with me for dinners when in town...these CEO's or Human Resource professionals would look down or away....

I shared my situation with one of my advisors and friend. He said, "it seems as though you and Mr. CEO are having an affair. Isn't that why he keeps meeting with you? You haven't worked with them for years." I listed with shock and unbelief at the conclusion because no matter what it seemed; **we never had an affair!**

I considered it from the outside looking in, "If she is so good and the CEO is publicly attributing his success to the coach he worked with, why have they not used her in any of their other offices, since?" Of course, I had asked myself the same question. But there was nothing else I could do to continue on my ambitious path than to take my client at face value and trust him.

Tier 1 prospective clients stopped engaging with my professional services. I could see the no-win situation I was in. IF I didn't keep meeting with Mr. CEO, whose mandate I delivered on, he told me I would no longer be considered professionally. If they never worked with me again, despite the substantiated results I delivered, my credibility and accomplishments would be dismissed and I would be seen as "just another coach."

However, by continuing to meet with him as he directed, and not be re-engaged professionally, all my claims of effectiveness were being dismissed anyways, and my kids and I were losing revenue. I couldn't seem to let myself accept that Mr. CEO had no intention of re-engaging me because I didn't want to "start over" and there was no reason for me to be denied. My options were limited, I had allowed my professional accomplishments to be overshadowed by the public suggestion that Mr. CEO and I were having an affair and if I didn't keep my hat in the right, it would appear we did have an affair. **We didn't!**

It seemed like I was watching a movie, not living my situation. How could this be happening to me, what had I done wrong?! I had earned the opportunity and professional credibility to continue my career of choice with Tier 1 clients. However, I couldn't move forward, and I wasn't willing to go backward. Either I would work with Tier 1's and continue on my path forward, or I would sell vacuum cleaners!

I finally just stopped pursuing Tier 1 companies to avoid being confronted with the same question and feeling cheap because the only crappy answer I had was: "He invites me to join him for dinners." Told me it was a short-term strategy, after all, I'm good, and deliver great results, these Tier 1 prospects could be revisited once they saw me working again with this global company.

In defeat, I let my income level drop, significantly. I was immobilized. Had no idea how to make sense of it all. Mr. CEO was still reaching out and scheduling meetings with me though, continually telling me to trust that he was looking into finding me more work, though the VP of HR, was flat out saying no, they've moved on. I guess that the VP of HR never knew that Mr. CEO was meeting with me, in fairly regular contact or that it was his Executive Assistant who would arrange the reservations for our dinner meetings, weeks before he came to Toronto. In our last dinner meeting, Mr. CEO began stroking my hand over dinner! Then, he took my hand in his and confessed personal feelings for me, asked me to engage in an affair with him, and meet him in Paris!

I had no idea how to process the whole situation, including his words; he's married, has two adult kids, plus, he's my client! My mind was racing, it all began to make sense: This is why he had never re-engaged me professionally! If I had still been a supplier and he sought to be involved with me, before enough years had passed to make it okay for such, Mr. CEO, would be in blatant violation of his own company's policy. Instead, he used his position of power to keep me engaged for all those years to proposition me and induce me to have sex with him. All my professional hopes, with his company and other multinationals, were annihilated! He had revealed his agenda, and his agenda was all about him, he didn't care about me or professional reciprocity or kindness. By "trusting" him, I had allowed my professional credibility to be cheapened and tainted in the eyes of others. His actions destroyed my professional opportunities, though I had advanced his.

My successful track record hinged almost exclusively on the 8 years with the CEO and this multinational, but now it was all for not in the eyes of prospects, and I was cheapened. Still even now, in prospecting for MaP Forward Inc., if I refer to the work I did with this multinational and CEO, am then asked about the subsequent work and their involvement in MaP Forward.... Naming the situation and offense makes him look bad, and surely cheapens me, so I just find a way around their question. It hurts me each time, and I know it's wrong, because I did serve my client and earned the privilege of reciprocity and we do live in a cause and effect world, and I love God, but we can't control how others choose to be.

By meeting with me so regularly, knowing he had no intent to re-engage me, Mr. CEO, ended up destroying my credibility as a powerful coach and very much violated HIS company policy. Not only are they a multinational, but they are also one of Canada's largest company's and proudest jewel, a company with an excellent reputation and and and....

A dog with a bone, naïve me, reached out again to the VP of HR. I made no mention of the words of love spoken, or of Mr. CEO's advance. I just told him that after all these years of meetings with Mr. CEO, but no work, I was in a very awkward position in the eyes of the market and the optics were ruining my professional credibility. I proposed a small contract with a local office, to eliminate any of the sinister suggestions, and enable me to walk away with my head high. Easy peasy. (Now I realize that another blind spot, besides my ambition, was my naiveite: not a good combination! I had exposed the policy abuse. The damage was done, and they needed me to be gone.)

Almost immediately, a stern response from the CEO!? He told me never to contact his company again. My former client, the VP of

Human Resources, had also been declared a satisfied client. His job description mandates that such issues be addressed by him, yet no professional courtesy was extended to me, not once did he reach out and address the issue... I was baffled! Mr. CEO's response was disproportionate to the suggestion/question posed and uncharacteristic of his personality profile, our ongoing professional relationship, and friendship. I'm thinking this is what a smoking gun looks like.

Part 2

I retained a lawyer and he contacted their head of legal and explained the whole situation. This head of legal has been named amongst the most progressive powerful women in Canada. Yet, she told us that they had researched my claims and decided, without asking me any question or having made any contact with me, there had been no improprieties. The VP of Communications issued me a falsified letter to be given to prospects who asked about the absence of ongoing work. The fact was, Mr. CEO was doing great things for their shareholders, I was an irrelevant nobody, an inconvenience, they brushed off.

I wanted their letter to work for me but couldn't use it because the facts had been fabricated. Nothing was aligning; they are amongst the top 200 most powerful companies in the world and have clear strict policies in place for such situations. But the "strict" policies didn't apply to the CEO. I understood. He was a huge value add for the company and its shareholders. Every member of the Executive team, including the Independent Chairman of the Board, got into action and moved to protect Mr. CEO. They refused to see his abuse of power. They too believed we had an affair and I was just being another scorned woman, and failing in business.

By now, I knew their policy well. The CEO had to silence me. His behavior was clearly in violation of many elements in his company's policy: no executive is to engage in conduct with suppliers that place any potential negative light on the supplier. All his public behaviors related to me though did precisely that, including his public declaration of my effectiveness because he said the words, requested meetings with me regularly though he had dropped me as a service provider...? Ironically, his publicly spoken kind words became the kiss of demise, and evidence of his duality with a service provider. But the reality is, no Corporate Governance or policy would ever favor a tiny supplier, like me, over an award-winning, highly respected CEO who is doing amazing things and earning huge returns for all. So, with my head hung low I retreated into my metaphorical cave, withdrew from the world, and with God's help, somehow raised my kids.

Part 3

When the #MeToo movement emerged, many years had already passed for me and the company had surely forgotten my inconvenient allegations. Though #MeToo, became an official "thing," I would not have sought to publicly hurt my client, the most powerful, award-winning businessperson in the country at the time! Regardless of how it played out for me personally, professionally, or financially his success story is a proud professional accomplishment for me.

The same lawyer who had approached them in the first attempt for justice and vindication, told me that he wanted to approach them as the hugely successful company they are and in light of the #MeToo movement, appeal to them on the grounds of social justice, business leadership, ethics, morality, and their reputation; he too had been taken aback by their initial response to my substantiated claims.

Though years had passed, mentally and emotionally, I was still devasted and actively trying to let this go, so I told him to do as he needed to do. When he told me, several months later, that he had sent their lawyer a letter, I did feel encouraged and believed that justice, in some form, would come. When the same lawyer told me, the following month, however, that they still hadn't even acknowledged his letter, I was so sad and hurt, again! They had blown him off and ignored *him; despite him appealing to their honor with truth, facts, evidence, and their policy which had been clearly violated by the same CEO, my client, who signed it.*

Their policy states:

1. Sexual harassment places a condition of employment ("keep meeting with me for dinner to advance your opportunities.")

2. No executive is to engage in conduct with suppliers that place any potential negative light on the supplier. All his public behaviors related to me created suspicion and suggested nefarious behavior on my part: His public declaration, endorsement of my effectiveness, commitment to ongoing work, and frequent meetings with me but never engaging my professional services again, though other coaches were working frequently and locally with his company.

3. Questions and discussions about a person's sexual life (for example, him asking me: "Did you have sexual relations with _____?")—**NO!**

4. Sexually touching a person (for example, taking my hand and caressing it).

5. Commenting on someone's sexual attractiveness—several examples, comments such as:

6. "You are gorgeous."

7. "You're so well dressed."

8. "You're like an amazon woman..."

9. Situations where there is unequal power between the people involved and is an attempt by one person to assert dominance over the other. The harassment can also occur when an individual is in a vulnerable position—several examples include:

10. "Let's switch to texting; don't email me anymore."

11. "You keep forgetting only to text me."

12. "On holidays with my family, thinking of you, don't respond."

13. "Keep meeting with me for dinner to advance your opportunities."
He continually insisted on a less formal professional relationship and I felt there was little room for me to speak up. Naturally, my interest was in building upon the success I had earned to advance my career and care for my family. It was as though he was testing me, laying the groundwork to see if I would respect his directives and allow him to set the tone.

My lawyer appealed to them on the grounds of #MeToo, a more just social and politically correct environment. Ignoring him was ignoring the true damages they caused me. How do these and other kinds of abuses of power, occur? Maybe that's why chairpersons and boards exist. NOPE, is all I can say to that! The Independent Chairman was complicit in the first substantiated claim and had blown us off. I doubt the board members even knew about my complaint against Mr. CEO.

When my lawyer told me his letter was ignored, I came out of my metaphorical cave. Feeling indignant about their indifference, I decided to reach out to a board member. I researched the board and reached out to the youngest female on their board, also a CEO. She forwarded my note to the Chair. This time, the Independent Chairman, directly reached out to me.

The company offered to hire the same investigator who declared "no improprieties," the first time. Finally, they hired different investigators. Near the end of the interview, during a break with just the female investigator, she spoke freely, forgetting the tape was still running, (I have a copy). She stated, in her opinion, the CEO's behavior was deplorable. She said, "you delivered. And his behavior was unjust!" She felt my substantiated claims, and the falsified letter from the VP of Communications was evidence of a cover-up. She spoke of her daughter, and that hearing my story made her scared for her daughter's future. Though the multinational/Defendant hired the investigator to establish their innocence, the investigator fingered them! However, that didn't matter, I was denied again!

The evidence, their policy, my substantiated claim, the mistruths in the VP of Communications letter, his suggestive romantic emails/texts, the dinner meetings his secretary arranged, paid for on company credit card; not even the investigator's opinion mattered. The Chairman sent me a closing letter, more or less stating, "the damages owed me would be too much, and he and the board have decided it was best to ignore me" and then the words, "We have concluded, no improprieties." When I asked him for transparency, a copy of the report, or an explanation to help me understand how my claim was dismissed, he declined and stated the case closed and blocked me from ever contacting his company again.

My guess is they weighed the odds; after all, I let it go once though my claims were clearly violations of their policy. I had no idea how to overcome the damage Mr. CEO caused to the career path I was on; optically the damage he caused me was irreparable. The CEO immediately retired.

Maybe they reasoned that even if I did speak up, nobody would care because the CEO had just announced his retirement, but maybe his retirement was unrelated to my allegations. All I know is that *our work together, earned him and his family well over 100 million dollars, by the time he retired.* I am still pleased that our work together was so successful for him. His success is proof to both he and I of my effectiveness as a high performance, results-focused coach! I recognize my blind spots, but, if I could do it all over, I would probably handle it the same way. I was fueled by my conviction and other values like courage, ambition, determination, results, vision, hope, faith, idealism, and faith. Sure, I got #Microed and taken off my chosen path but it never felt like a risk, and there was so much more to gain by leading with Faith and Trusting; after all, it could have played out as the Law of Cause and Effect promises. While it didn't play out that way, that is on Mr. CEO, the Chairman, the Head of Legal, the VP of Communications, the VP of HR, the incoming President/CEO, and the Board Member.

Though I didn't have the support or insight to know how to make things better, there is no doubt in my mind, thoughtful sophistication served me. Tapping into key values like courage and confidence enabled me to swim for many years with the sharks and make a name for myself professionally, and elevated my kids and me, financially. It was the profile with its scientific validity, which assured me that this too would pass, I would stay standing and recover mentally and emotionally. After the first failed attempt at justice, I did take a job selling vacuum cleaners, because all my previous visions were no longer, and I just needed to prove to myself that I could move on and start over. I didn't stay in the job long. Sage, my daughter, told me to quit because every day before going to work, I would cry. Through it all, my Faith sustained us. We didn't have to sell the house, nor was I required to send my children away from me to live with their dad.

> *"And we know that God causes everything to work together for the good of those who love God and are called according to his purpose for them." Romans 8:28 (NLT)*

We are all at the mercy of life; and as such, there will be problems and challenges along the way. Thoughtful sophistication, personal mastery, self-awareness, won't change that. It will, however, help us remember that we get to choose to come out even stronger. It has been said, **"eighty percent of success is showing up."**

PART 2
Focus

Self-Awareness
+ **Focus**
+ Strategy
= SUCCESS

Chapter 5

Success Triggers

The world favors those who actively focus on the process of their own lives. Focus is the second part of my success formula and the topic of this part of *K.I.S.S.* I'm not talking about SMART goals—you know, goals that are Specific, Measurable, Attainable, Realistic, and Timely. I'm talking about the kind of focus that you feel when they are truly interested in a pursuit, not because you have to be, or because you feel you should, but because the objects of your focus are meaningful, exciting, and motivating, for you! Focus is an action-orientated function that creates results. Of course, though, sometimes, the actions related to focus do not always translate, as fast as we'd like, into visible results.

I make lots of reference to values in our discussion of self-awareness (thoughtful sophistication), Part 1, but now let's focus more tightly on "Values." Our values are our feelings, and the more we understand them, the higher our emotional intelligence. You already know your feelings matter, and as you already know, you cherish some feelings more than others. It is the feelings you cherish and want more of which I invite you to focus on. i.e., feelings like joy, happiness, motivation, inspiration, stimulation, etc. Focus on them as feelings and focus on them as concepts. For example, feel/be, joyous. **Also**, notice, acknowledge, try to understand, what about the particular situation or person or job, is contributing to your feeling of Joy. Knowing what brings you joy, enables you to find more opportunities, people, or jobs to target and have more joy, in your life! Another example of a value is Justice. Justice, however, isn't a feeling, it is a conceptual value. You will either notice and care if justice is present, or you won't. For some of us, Justice, as a value is important, for others, not. There is nothing to be judged about another values, or your values. We each have been hardwired with unique personalities and values that inform our path forward. These values exist as random pieces of a puzzle until we put the puzzle together. We already know, even if we don't really understand its profound influence, self-awareness is one of the foundations required for a meaningful, fulfilling successful life. Self-awareness includes emotional intelligence. Emotional intelligence is how we learn to validate emotions; emotional intelligence helps us better understand the emotions of the people around us. Self-awareness involves knowing how to identify the causes that produce your best most fulfilling results and using that knowledge to inform you of the best way to respond and direct your emotions for optimal outcomes for yourself and in your life! With time and persistence, it is possible to control your emotions, feelings = values, and direct them towards better results; body, mind, and soul.

We've already established that most individuals go through their lives without self-awareness, self-understanding, and don't pay much attention to their emotions, feelings = values. Most either completely ignore their emotions, feelings = values, or let their emotions, feelings chaotically control their lives. Emotions are a powerful force that can produce miracles in our lives, or completely ruin them.

The self-awareness you are gaining is to empower and inform your mind. As you learn to identify, acknowledge, and spot your values, their presence, or their lack of presence, the more success you have. Self-awareness is the buffer between our emotions, feelings = values, and our reactions. The more you develop your thoughtful sophistication in this way the more control you have over your life results. This guide is to show you how to be and feel sexier and more successful. Take the time to identify and acknowledge what makes you happy. Then look out for and target more opportunities, people, or jobs that make you feel happy; doing so will help you have more happiness in your life! We can add pieces, emotions that we want, to the values puzzle but we cannot remove or chose to ignore, and still have a fulfilling, successful life, any of the values we've been assigned. We all are required to be who we have been hardwired to be. Your reward for being who you have been created to be is your Throne, and all you have to do to claim your Throne is complete your values puzzle. The more you know and celebrate the values that energize you and make you feel alive, the more successful and fun your journey! You have every opportunity to make your life an exciting, daring, adventure, and experience! If there is a demotivating and energy-draining value amongst your pieces, know that it is out of place. Get it out of your puzzle/experience, fast! But first, seek to understand what about that piece (a situation, conversation, or job) makes it unwanted. Is it the way you are being spoken to, is it the content of what is being said about you, is it related to the nature of the job, is it the style of communication, or the lack of sensitivity, clarity, respect, or motivation or or or? Generally speaking, the value that we are seeking can be found in what we are disliking. For example, if we are feeling disrespected…safe to say the value we want to be feeling is, "respect." If so, make a conscious point of only engaging when you feel the presence of "respect." Remember, you can add new different and uplifting values, you just can't remove an assigned value, when we ignore or neglect an assigned value, we feel empty. Honor your values! Make your choices focused on the values which jive with who you are, and make you feel great!

What to Focus On

It's easy, intellectually, to understand how focused energy translates into great returns, but it's not so clear where and how to best focus that energy. That is the experience of living: Risk is involved. Risk, and experiment, intelligently. If you know/sense something or someone is not "right" for your objective at hand, heed the warning and spare yourself. I encourage you to risk with a focus on your existing values, and add other exciting, meaningful values as you live your excellent adventure!

It is the presence of personally motivating values that add to our success. If you find yourself in roles, personally or professionally, that do not incorporate or allow for you to factor in your key values and motivators; you are misaligned and won't create valuable results. Move on. You have no room in your values puzzle, or life, for mediocrity. You have a Throne to claim.

Reframe the Risk

We can choose to be guided, influenced, and directed by others, or we can risk, be self-directed, and trust our values. Maxine is an excellent example of someone who ultimately decided to maximize her potential and risk.

Maxine was perplexed regarding the origin of her fundamental values. She was bored with her life and wanted not to be. Maxine had been emulating the values she had grown up with and observed around her. She was frustrated with her efforts and attempts to improve her life. She recognized that some kind of pattern interrupt was necessary to reframe her situation. She decided that she wanted a re-do, and decided to see how things would look if she led with her values. Ultimately, Maxine chose to look at her life, situations, and choices differently. She had always loved God but in a passive kind of way. She told me, "If my values are from God then leading with them should be easy. At least easier than feeling so restless." This revelation started a chain reaction of success in Maxine's life.

Values, like risk orientation a value, are amongst the spiritual DNA God gives us to realize our visions. We each represent a unique element of God; our values are how He develops a personal relationship with each of us. When we reject the values, He handpicked for us; we reject Him and His vision for our lives. That makes him sad. Let us honor God by becoming the person He designed each of us to be.

Values are more than just good, noble words we pick off a menu. We may find our values by making the wrong choices and feeling a dis-ease. Maybe you have a dis-ease, a sense you aren't living your values with the degree of conviction you want, out of fear for how it could play out, or because you don't know-how. It doesn't matter "why," and you alone must live with the consequences of your choice. When we allow our convictions, actions, and, or approach to life to be dictated to us by others we are compromising, dare say, selling out on ourselves, playing small.

You are a Queen, live in such a way as to claim your Throne!

When you honor your values and let them guide your focus, you live and have a successful life. It can be no other way. Never forget, your best is still ahead of you. Be willing to risk for it. We all take risks, in varying degrees. Maybe you don't recognize your comfort and ability to risk, so step back and let yourself remember the successful risks you've already taken. Everything we do, from baking a cake, *will it be tasty*, to developing a pitch, *will it be well received*, to going after a big client, *will you get the client, will you have the funds to cover your expenses, will you get the job you've applied for,* and there's even risk in needing others, *will I receive the help I need, or not?* Sometimes our risks are rewarded, other times not. That is just the nature of life.

For the world to continue advancing in progressive, exciting new ways-risk-takers are required. When we advance as individuals, we advance the world. How cool is that! To be amongst this group requires only that you choose, daily, to honor your success triggers (your values). Each day declare that "today you will be true to your values," pick a new one each day and track how often you lead with it that day, notice how your risk played out. That's all you have to do. Daily, incorporate another value that motivates you. Living this way is the best, and easiest, type of risk to take, even though all you will be doing is honoring your success triggers. *Where's the risk in that?*

To understand and focus on your potential you may be required to risk for the unknown. There is no reward without risk; a truth that cannot be changed! However, what does change with each courageous step you take forward towards your Throne, is that everything gets easier. Your unfolding is enabled by the accumulation of small steps and big steps. When a risk feels too hard or intimidating, step back and reframe the "risk."

Sarah was an excellent example of this:

Sarah knew she was frustrated, bored, and not challenged doing what she was doing as an accountant. With two kids and a mortgage though, she needed to be stable, and make good money. Except, she wanted more for her life because she felt like she was just existing. She knew she wasn't fulfilled. She needed the security her job provided: she felt stuck. Sarah decided to work with me and do a profile of her personality. Her profile showed her what she needed to be mindful of if she was to be successful in the small business she wanted to build. She acknowledged there would be challenges for her. Sarah minimized her risks by focusing on her potential as per her scientifically validated and objective personal assessment. Her values, fortunately for her, mostly supported her personality profile. She boldly looked at the two options in front of her: stay put, have her steady paycheck, and be dissatisfied or take more control over her life and advance what she had the potential to have. Both options were risky to her because both options had their challenges. She decided to leave her job and focus on her values. It wasn't an easy decision for her to make, but she did and was joyous, happy, and felt so empowered by her potential. She saved and used that time to develop her strategy; she met the most necessary of her obligations and kept her focus on her big picture. Sarah knew that she was taking a calculated risk on herself and actually felt rejuvenated by her courage. Being fulfilled doesn't always mean having it all in the way society measures, though it can. When we choose fulfillment as our primary objective, it is easier to live our values and be successful. It's as though we are saying to life, "okay, I accept however this plays out, but I'm going for it." Sarah, a Christian, loved the Lord and focused on His promise to her:

> *"In all your ways, acknowledge Him, and He will make straight your paths." Proverbs 3:6 (ESV)*

Sarah's example proves that the best ROI in these times is to stay focused on the "why" we would be willing to take unnecessary risks. She had to stay in the "waiting place" for longer than she wanted, but she used that time to plan, strategize, pray and identify which values she needed to have front and center in her life. She focused on keeping her sanity and courage, as she stayed in faith. Hers was a great strategy for her. Find ways to keep your sanity and courage. Focus on how not to panic, or feel desperate, or think you are alone to claim your Throne. Take your mind OFF things when the waiting feels like it is taking too long, or that the funds are running low. Journal, workout, cry, freak out, get sad, find inspiration, read about God, read the Bible, go for a walk, listen to music, and, or find others to focus on and help. Waiting is an uncomfortable process, and sometimes it will feel harder than others. If you keep your commitment to focus on your vision though, you will move closer than you've ever been, to your Throne!

It's natural to want more control and make things happen, and sometimes our efforts will play out and maybe even be good enough, but you are too good for only good enough. It is entirely possible for you to have an exceptional experience, and of that, you are worthy! Sometimes, I find the best strategy is to do nothing. I now know, it is best to get out of God's way, so He has space to fulfill His promises and BE God. We each have to decide, daily, to "trust more than we control." This, of course, is not at all easy for those of us who prefer and seek control! If you can relate to wanting control, the only and best thing to do is force yourself to take the foot off the gas pedal in your own life. It can feel scary, especially with your eyes open, but it will net you your best return on effort! Stay focused on all the greatness planned for you!

> *"I know the plans I have for you,"* declares the LORD,
> *"plans to prosper you and not to harm you, plans to
> give you hope and a future." Jeremiah 29:11 (NIV)*

Sometimes, just living and having to figure things out, feels scary and the idea of stretching further than you've ever stretched may feel downright mortifying. However, that's life. Control the variables you can; increase your thoughtful sophistication and develop your faith! The best fruit is at the top of the tree, so if you want the best, you will be required to stretch. Develop your Faith, and use sophistication, as your ladder! Or live your life the way you always have.

Chapter 6
The Values Mandate—Exercises

K nowing your values is key. Their real power shows itself when you dare to live them! Awareness and application of your values gives you a strategic advantage, enabling you to win on your terms, in all of your roles.

Understand, I mean, really get this: others have different values than you and me. As a result, we won't usually really know why others may be acting in their unique ways and why things are playing out as they are. As your thoughtful sophistication becomes unshakeable, you'll naturally look for the values at play in others; by doing so, you communicate better with them, have better relationships, and improve upon your results!

The more you engage your unique, maybe even quirky values, the more satisfaction, success, and sexiness you have. The one mandate we each have been given for our lives is to honor our values; each of us must choose whether we accept this mandate or not.

Identify Your Must-Have Values

The following are questions that you have all the answers to. Answering them will help you identify some of your must-have values and open your mind to feelings you may have rejected not knowing they were "values."

Think back to times when you didn't realize the success you were seeking. What was missing, that if present, may have helped you achieve better success? Don't just say, "it wasn't a fit," while that may be true, ask yourself, why it wasn't a fit. If this involves a specific relationship, what was the feeling that person enabled in you or brought out in you? Next, consider some of your best moments. What feelings were you feeling? Which of those feelings do you want more of in your life?

Now give thought to what made one of your worst moments so bad. What specific feeling did that prompt in you? What feelings or values did you feel you were being forced to sacrifice or felt like were being denied to you? Not all feelings are values to be pursued. For example, guilt is not a value. Guilt is a form of manipulation that comes as a result of not kowtowing to other people's agendas. We're not naturally hardwired to feel guilty. Only consider energizing feelings. The key is you identify the values that make you feel most alive.

All values are of God's perfect character. We each have values that have been handpicked uniquely for the purposes He has assigned for each of us. As such, your unique values, her unique values, and his unique values are great. Focus on finding the values that you have been uniquely assigned. Knowing, pursuing, and living your greatness with your unique values assures you of a life filled with **inspiration!** You will never play it safe, or small again! Personal safety is not a value to aspire for because it keeps us small. To care about and focus on advancing the safety of others, however, offers increase. Do more **"due-diligence"** to understand your values and the opportunity they offer you for abundance, opulence, and joy. Once you feel confident and clear about your values and purpose take more **"risks"** this is an excellent one-two combo that produces **"motivation."** Within the list of values available to you, favor the values that are **"growth-inducing,"** notice how your spirit will direct you. Remember, you are not doing this alone.

"I will instruct you and teach you in the way you should go; I will counsel you with my eye upon you." Psalm 32:8 (ESV)

Go back to your list of values and divide your list under the headings of must-have values and nice-to-have values. If you're okay with only a little bit of fun in your life, then "fun" is not a must-have value for you. If you know you want to always have **"compassion"** or **"family"** in your life, then make your choices, accordingly, ensure your must-have values can always be active and present in your life. Let yourself openly acknowledge what values you most cherish and want. If you notice you enjoy being part of a **"team,"** or value **"community"** ensure those values are present.

If you notice you get bored unless you're creative or **"stimulated,"** make **"creativity"** and **"stimulation"** standards of engagement for you: if you can't see the promise of their presence, don't engage. Ask better more specific questions, to establish the likelihood of your values being present. **"Hope,"** is a wonderful value to lead with. Establish if you truly see hope in the current approach, situation, or relationship. Seek **"reciprocity,"** and **"respect."** Remember. your choices impact others too. As much as possible, but not at the expense of your Throne, always show kindness to others. Save yourself and others time, and **"energy,"** and avoid making too many uninformed choices, unless it is just the nature of the situation and such **"risk-taking"** is required. Handle all your **"relationships,"** as you want to be treated.

You may be living many of your values already, lucky you! The more values you claim, the more you will enhance the quality of your effectiveness, sexiness, and success as a human being. I keep repeating variations of the same point because it bears reiterating. Your values are your guide and sometimes to honor them, it may be necessary to say, "screw practicality," in favor of your mandate: You are here to claim your Throne.

Everyone benefits when you live your values; after all, that is when you are your best; productive, happy, and successful! Don't tolerate being okay with the presence of a whole lot of nice-to-have values, focus on the quality of your values, not the quantity. Stay vigilant. Keep the focus on your personal **"vision,"** your values are the ticket for **"sustainable engagement"** and excellence! You are now changing lanes, from good to great, and the more values you identify as **motivating**, the easier it is to achieve your transformation! Identify no less than ten values.

*Robin is an excellent example of someone whose vision was easier to advance just by getting in touch with her values. She had been downsized and taken off her career path from her job as a senior sales executive and that is when she and I met. She wanted to find work outside the field of sales and still make a decent living. She was ready for something new and different. She had never felt much passion in sales, but she didn't know what line of work would spark **passion** in her.*

*I asked her about times in her past when she did feel passionate. Robin came alive when she talked about **music**. She had wanted to **study** composition and had a promising start as a pianist, but it wasn't practical. She was told she had to be **responsible** and focus on what kind of living that would produce for her, as a woman, and as an eventual wife and mother. So, she did what she needed to do to generate a "good" living. She was saddened when she talked about the values that she had forfeited by abandoning her love for music. She decided to carve out space in her house for a music room and started working on some new compositions. She **courageously** took*

action and **risked** by putting out an ad to find, musicians interested in working together on contemporary compositions. Her ad received responses, and she ended up forming an ensemble. She was surprised at the **energy** this gave her to find other things that **jazzed** her. She ended up taking a course that allowed her to **learn** and find a **leadership** role in the music industry. Her new job kept her still involved in sales, but she said that "selling something she cared about reminded her how **fun** sales could be."

Our passions can get squeezed out subtly or overtly, we can be talked out of our dreams, or maybe we can't see how our dreams could work. Just keep your focus on the light, let yourself be drawn to the energy. Your Throne is yours to claim.

> *"You, LORD, keep my lamp burning; my God turns*
> *my darkness into light." Psalm 18:28 (NIV)*

Going along to get along can work for those whose values are other-centric. If values such as **"nobility"** and **"selflessness"** are essential to you, then stay focused on others. If such values don't energize you, then consider finding the values that do, and live to honor them. There's no nobility in making others or family your focus if what you are really doing is avoiding the search for your drivers.

Values in Action

At times, we are required to engage in activities not related to our list of values. Stray from your primary values, if you choose to, and do it in awareness, with your eyes wide open and only in moderation. Otherwise, your must-haves will be swamped by your nice-to-haves, and you'll be living your life more for others than yourself, if you have a value around **self-sacrifice**, then keep going. Try to hold yourself to the values that appear on your must-have's list.

When Isabelle focuses more on the experiences/feelings/values she wants to have and makes decisions based on them; she achieves better results. She has peace of mind. Moreover, she is a better person and mother for it.

For Alexa:

*Alexa values **boldness**, in herself and others. She wants her thoughts and actions to reflect this in respectful ways. Boldness is a value, not a need. Needs are about existing, just like food is a need to live. Without boldness, Alexa will not perish. However, with boldness, she has more fulfillment in her life. Upon deciding she would be bolder, she began to come to life, it was fun for her, and she embraced risks less cautiously.*

Boldness is about a feeling, a desire, and a mindset fueled by *possibilities*. Our personalities and values work together to help make life easier; we don't have to make ourselves focus on what comes naturally to us. Remember Gurpreet? When our focus is on doing what we already do well, without acknowledging or just ignoring how we feel along the way, our results are mediocre. We may be "good" at what we are doing, and our aptitudes may be engaged BUT, when we "do" without feeling good or great, we become like robots empty and boring. Boredom is a killer: it kills relationships, potential, and people. You are equipped to realize every objective you have, either in your personality or by way of your values. You have everything to gain by increasing your self-awareness.

Erin provides another example:

Erin thought that values were just words; words people thought were noble or good because often that is how values are presented. Upon discovering her values, she was both elated and scared. The exercise enabled her to recognize that she hadn't been living her values, and that was why she didn't feel at peace or have better results.

There was much misalignment in her life. Every day felt the same, like in the movie "Groundhog Day." Erin wasn't happy or satisfied with her life. She didn't want to have to make the choices she did, and at the same time, she knew it wasn't about playing it safe anymore. Erin had kids. She wanted to lead them by an example she believed in. She wanted to feel good, happy, successful, and in alignment with her life. She did believe God loved her, is compassionate and has a plan for her. She knew that she had made too many of her critical choices without any real sense of anything; who she was, what she wanted. Once Erin decided she wanted to live the remainder of her life on her terms and by her values, she took definitive action, left her job, and ended her marriage. Many of us are like Erin, willing to live a life of compromise, at the expense of a quality existence. Until we find the courage to say, "no more."

Don, a senior executive I worked with for several years once told me, "There are two types of fighter pilots in the world: old fighter pilots and bold fighter pilots—but there are never old and bold fighter pilots." Which kind of fighter pilot will you be? Decide now and focus on aligning your choices to reflect the kind of life you want to live.

Personality Traits and Values

As we covered in Section 1, each of us has a unique set of personality traits and, generally speaking, our values extend from our personality. For example, for those of you with a "big pictured" personality trait, not generally too concerned with details, it is likely that you have values around, "exploration," or "possibilities." However, it is possible and still perfect to not be big pictured and still value "exploration," or "possibilities," it's just not as common. When values are a new concept, in my experience, knowing our personality traits enables us to more easily identify our values. The more we understand the potential in our personality and processing style, naturally we learn to set ourselves up for success!

Use your feelings, values, to guide your focus. Focus on what truly interests you, feels good, and motivates you to claim your Throne as the Queen of You. What you focus on, is what becomes your reality. To change your reality, shift your focus.

You may be thinking, "yeah sure, if it was only that easy." It is that easy to acknowledge your feelings, the only effort required is that you choose to feel energized! With this kind of conscious intentionality, you courageously let your feelings dictate your next steps. I know it could feel like a bold way to approach life; but is it, really? For example, if you feel good, excited, interested, or curious about something or someone—keep going. If you notice that your energy is zapped, abort. Stay focused on your energizing values, whatever they are. The effort required is an easy effort when you know what you are working towards, and what values you want to be guided by. Ask yourself how badly you want "more" for yourself. If your conviction for that reality is not yet strong, though, or the results are not forthcoming, it may be tempting to abandon the idea of your vision. Don't. Your conviction is simply being tested; how bad do you want what you want. Queens have much privilege and power, the Universe needs to be sure you are ready for your Throne. Be prepared, stay committed to your destiny, trust you will be guided, keep the course, and accept that the journey forward is rarely linear. Do this, and you will realize success. I know it feels risky and ridiculous to believe that success could be achieved this way, but what else are our feelings for, if not to guide us? You have everything you need, by way of your values and your personality, to have the life you were meant to live. I've shared scriptures with you, promises God has made to each of us, and remind you that along with the unique values He has assigned you, you will not, cannot fail.

"Let us not become weary in doing good, for at the proper time we will reap a harvest if we do not give up." Galatians 6:9 (NIV)

You are your key to abundance, joy, success, and sexiness!

Meet Stephanie

When Stephanie chose to act on this truth it made an incredible difference in her quality of existence! Stephanie loved the idea of focusing on her essence; the idea deeply resonated with her, it just felt right. However, she had an affinity for control and was effective at producing her desired outcomes in the professional situations she was in. She had developed a system and it worked for her, as long as she did certain things in certain ways. At the same time, her love of control didn't leave much room for her to be curious about her essence. Even though when she made time for her MaP Forward program and allowed herself to consider the whole concept of values, faith, and vision and they seemed so airy-fairy, to her logical mind, she kept showing up. She read her profile and resumed living life the way she was accustomed to functioning. She felt her intuition directing her to consider her profile more, but it was just a function of AI, with some interesting graphs. Her intellect told her to maintain focus on what she knew mostly worked, so that's what she did, she kept her focus on controlling; for good or bad, she at least could see her actions play out, and sometimes it worked, others times it didn't. That's life, she was cool with that.

The prospect of trusting her feelings, which as a rule of thumb, she didn't often consider, intrigued her. But she preferred the concrete. While she didn't value her feelings much, she was open to the idea of, at least, noticing them. By doing so, though, she was surprised how it helped her notice and look for energizing feelings: when she felt energized and when she didn't. Stephanie was surprised that her feelings offered her useful intel, she became somewhat curious about that. She was amazed at how liberated she was slowly starting to feel like she could relax a little and listen to her feelings. What pleased her the most was that by listening to her feelings, she was able to control even better. "Who knew" emotions could be so useful, she said. Her parents always downplayed the need for her to be passionate about her work. Her dad often said to her, "Do you think I enjoy what I'm doing? I'm doing it for the family." She was told to focus on making the right amount of money to support her lifestyle, not give thought to how she felt about it. Intellectually, she found it illogical to use her feelings to direct her, but she was enjoying her experiment with them. She slowly made herself stop being concerned about how others responded to her choices, knowing they didn't know or feel, what she was feeling. To stop consulting with others, was hard for her, as she is a relationship orientated woman and as such, thought she was "supposed" to seek others validation. Stephanie, in her experimentation mode, decided to be more intentional about with whom she shared, to have a true perspective. Rather than continue asking people like her dad, who never considered his feelings, she sought out people whom she respected and did acknowledge their feelings. Stephanie was relieved of the feelings of guilt she didn't even realize she was living with and said that without guilt, she felt lighter and more able to focus on living her life. Stephanie found her personal values by focusing on her feelings.

Stephanie chose to understand how to use her unique set of motivators—values, feelings, to achieve success, on her terms. Her approach can work for all of us. Travel only on the paths you enjoy, focus on your God-given values, and realize the abundance that awaits you! Live your values, be a magnet for the opportunities you seek, and along the way, be an inspiration for others!

Meet Joanne

Joanne never understood why she was driven by values that she never observed growing up or was taught to value. Things like adventure, risk, relationships, and variety were not a part of her upbringing. She always thought she was to follow the values her mom taught her, routine, stability, and harmony, though she sensed they were holding her back, she knew she had more to offer than these values that were keeping her small. Still, without any tangible reason to live her own unique values, she lived the way she was taught. She tried to make herself accept that her life was just meant to be how it was, a boring one. However, she couldn't help but question if there was more to life. As Joanne began to consider the things that she noticed gave her energy and made her feel excited and happy, she noticed she felt anxiety, her sense of self was shaken. She decided she preferred the safety of what she knew and rejected the feelings that didn't align with how she had been living. She didn't want to rock the boat of her life and told herself it was better to focus on ensuring everyone was happy, agreed, and got along. She knew she wanted adventure in her life, but Joanne also knew that the concept of the unknown was uncomfortable and felt unsafe. She wanted a more enjoyable life, but without ambiguity or risk. She tried to again, dismiss her feelings, and thought she could just put her feelings to the side. Round and round she went, telling herself there was no reason for her to explore a different reality, professionally, her focus was on being a good manager; she looked at things very practically and the path she was on was working. Her mom was proud of her, she made a good income, why did her feelings "have to" matter. Her company hired my company, to prepare her for her next position, she completed her profile and was introduced to the concept of values. She was surprised how none of the values she was told to embrace and live by, actually inspired her or felt natural, and her profile helped her understand why. She couldn't understand how her values were so different from her upbringing. She knew she wanted her life to be exciting, full of discovery, and opportunity and that she was curious about many things. But she had spent 33 years telling herself everybody wants that kind of life, and the best, most reliable decisions were the ones guided by practicality, not feelings or emotion. Once she considered the truth of her design and nature, she *became finally committed to finding more personal satisfaction and success in her career!*

Bottom line: Trust your feelings.

Honoring Your Values

It's easy to focus only one value or perspective, apart from there being no growth in such an approach, such a limited focus renders us boring and indecisive! If you value **nurturing**, do not make your life only about that and still expect interesting people to be drawn to you. Unless that is, you don't have a value or need for **interesting** people as long as you're able to nurture. Just be fair to yourself and those around you. Don't hold it against your partner or others if they don't value what you value. If that is the case, be sure to surround yourself with enough people who do value what you value, so you, too, feel valued.

The nurture value was used for illustrative purposes, nurturing could be replaced by any value. For example, if your partner loves achieving tangible results, recognize they must be true to their design. It's possible to not like how others choose to direct their energy, and that's your issue, not theirs. Be wiser and ensure your choices in life, work and play, align with your values, and the values with your work or those whom you are closest—alignment impacts the quality of your experiences.

Certain values will not necessarily help you be more successful per se, in a corporate role. However, when "less business-like" types of values energize you and you want to lead with them more, consider industries or roles or business opportunities that allow you to leverage your excellence! If you value **integrity**, which is about believing in what you believe, then you're being called to move past good to great. When integrity is a must-have value, know that it is natural to do a deeper level of due diligence about the people, places, or things that will most support your transformation!

There is and always will be a correlation between your success and the presence of your main values. Don't try to make yourself value something you don't, you will only be adding stress to your life, being fake, and lacking integrity. No one else can truly dictate to you, what to value, what others try to mandate on us, are "shoulds." Just because you are made to think you "should" do something, that doesn't mean you must. Ask yourself what you most want to feel and have and then identify which values will get you to your desired state. If you want help to understand any of these concepts more sign up for our 4-week online course, "Self-Awareness for Success," www.mapforward.org/success.

Values Are Everything

Make a conscious effort to live the feelings, values, and behaviors which inspire you. Girlfriend, you've got places to go and people to see: Your Throne that has been prepared and is waiting for you. Don't delay realizing your destiny and potential any longer. Follow your values.

There have been times, like with Joanne, when profiles have proven the nature vs. nurture debate is very real. The profiles capture our personality, usually a function of our nurturing. Our nature is a function of the specific values we have been assigned. Your values are your values. They may not speak to me in the same way as they speak to you, just like my values may not inspire you as they inspire me. And that's okay. Both personality and values differences explain why people think differently, and may have two very different responses to the same questions or opportunities in life. Life imitates art though, and value is in the eye of the beholder. It is possible, even likely, that you'll find yourself having to choose between either your personality or your values. Your values are unfettered and directly given to you from God so you can claim your Throne. My vote and advice to you will always be to favor your values over your personality. Your values are everything!

Pursue as many values as you choose, despite how the world positions it, financial success and fulfillment, for example, do not have to be an either, or proposition. If it feels possible, it is, pursue both. On my internet TV show, I ask my successful, accomplished, powerful guests if it was their self-awareness that enabled their success, or if it was their success that led to self-awareness. Once upon a time, it was the latter, for most. However, by the time joy enabling self-awareness is garnered, it is not obvious or easy for deeply entangled lives to truly manage the truth of who they are and ride the wave. Thankfully today, as the collective consciousness rises, more of us are achieving success and fulfillment with the help of our thoughtful sophistication; before our lives get too entangled. I remind my son, who is starting his second year of university, during a pandemic, **the Dalai Lama drives a Mercedes**. Test the hypothesis for yourself.

Meet Sally

Sally decided she would live a life on her terms and follow her values. She told herself, therefore, she could never be rich, and was at peace with that. Sally mostly enjoyed her life, and if it wasn't for the constant state of debt, she found herself in, her focus would have been more inspiring. I respected Sally's decision to live a life on her terms, without compromise, and wished she hadn't convinced herself that it would be without ever having enough money. She was an entrepreneur and a sought after professional, and that was enough for her. Sally frequently underpriced her services as a creative though she produced excellent work. She grew up seeing her parent's relationship with money. Sally unconsciously internalized the notion that money was a bad thing. As the dutiful daughter she is, she rejects money though she loves what it does for her. She is trapped by nothing more than the scarcity mentality she learned as a child. She learned to reject the premise that God designed us to enjoy the abundance He has enabled us to have. *Thankfully, she decided to achieve transformation and focused on reframing her perspective to one of abundance.*

Though it's not usually "fast," it could be, with conscious intentionality. I have yet to find a more rewarding, fulfilling, and successful approach to life than leading and living my values, playing to my strengths, and praying. The same approach could work for us all. Though I am not good at waiting, and not all my efforts and hopes work out, immediately; I do feel a deep immense joy in knowing I walk by Faith.

> *"You can pray for anything, and if you have faith, you will receive it." Matthew 21:22 (NLT)*

Don't reject these truths because they seem too easy. Life wasn't meant to be hard.

Chapter 7

Power of Refocus

Meet Jane

Jane was 48 when she left her marriage; she had been an executive at a privately-owned family-run business. Her identity had been primarily tied up with her role because it gave her high visibility and a good reputation. Jane was a consummate professional and had been living that life for almost 20 years but felt her life too stayed. She had no idea that her decision to leave her husband would end up costing her her job.

She is an optimist and thought the job loss would be negligible because she was a great worker and figured her reputation would assure her of even better opportunities. She focused, as any of us would, on controlling her results. Unfortunately for her, things did not play out as she had expected, earned, or deserved. Years later, her

85

life was nowhere close to being how things once were. Jane had to refocus and didn't know how to, or where to begin. After spending some time with her, she began to create a strategy that would help her refocus and win in life!

Situations like Jane's make it easy for us women to get bitter and cynical, even though we know these low energy-producing emotions keep us down. We already know that, sometimes, our efforts to move forward in life are mistreated or denied to us by others. When and if that happens to you, I'm sorry. I know it can be immobilizing. Do what you can to stay high level. Reframe your perception of the situation to enable you to tap into more positive energy and recognize which values enable you a better, different attitude. Of course, yuck is yuck, until it stops being yuck. But the tides will change, it is a law of the Universe. Sometimes, all that is required is to look at the situation differently, reframe it in such a way as to enable you to lead with faith; believe, trust and know that God will find a way to use your setbacks, challenges, and disappointment to your advantage.

Whether you are the working woman who doesn't want to get out of bed when her alarm goes off, or the mom who feels like she has nothing left to give, or the wife who can't live up to everyone's standards, or the woman who is agonizing over the challenges in her life, or the woman living alone, or woman who takes Valium for panic attacks, or the woman who can't hold down a job; our weak and vulnerable state does nothing to repel God from us. **He is drawn to our weakness**. A desire for Him will bring Him closer to you, and you closer to Him.

> *"He gives power to the weak and strength to the powerless... those who trust in the Lord will find new strength." Isaiah 40:29–31 (NLT)*

Meet Julie

Julie came to MaP Forward because she wanted to have hope in better days, but she felt her life had been put on hold. Her life had been challenging almost from the start with parental issues and a sad upbringing. Julie left home, married, and had kids with an abusive man. She ended the marriage with courage and determination to have the kind of life she felt she is meant to live. She tried many things to improve upon her career success and to find a new partner. She knew her destiny was bigger and better than the life she had always known and just felt so discouraged by her past. Her efforts to realize her vision played out well enough for her, and it was almost enough. But she wasn't happy. Julie felt as if the world was against her, and that life would always be an uphill battle. She tried to be practical, maybe too practical. Later, when Julie started listening to her feelings and her intuition, she began to have more hope. Currently, Julie is writing a book about her life, and though she is not yet done and has no plans for it, she is elated with herself. She focused on her feelings, and that seems to have opened her mind to exploring new possibilities!

Consider Melissa and Tina

Melissa's challenge was that she had the weight of the world on her shoulders and would rarely take the time to be still, and care for herself. She was always so busy trying to be in control, organizing things in her life to allow for no surprises. She was consistently exhausted and approaching "burn out." Melissa had a nervous breakdown and was forced to surrender. Consequently, after resting for a few weeks and resuming life at a slower pace, she began asking herself how she could be handling her life with less effort and stress. She began releasing the need to be in constant control and see what that would produce.

Though she didn't much care about how she felt and didn't have much interest in her values, directly, her breakdown forced her to step back and consider her life from a different perspective. That is when we introduced the concept of values more clearly to her and positioned them in the context of results since our values ultimately are always leading us to a specific result, experience, or ultimate feeling. This perspective on values excited her! She loved the idea of being more effective and successful, just by being intentional about living her values. She realized she could afford to Trust more, and not always control.

Meet Tina, her values are in bold, notice how they play out when applied.

Tina knew she was not feeling **excited** about her life, but she also knew she liked to feel **safe**. She even knew that while she wanted to feel safe and not rock the boat too much, she wanted to be **inspired** day-to-day. Tina knew when her pursuits were **challenging**, **meaningful**, and had an element of **adventure/risk** to them; she was **engaged**, and **motivated**, **excited** to be alive. She knew she enjoyed being **passionate and bold**—that the bolder she could be, the more open she was to **learn** new things, and the more **invigorated** she felt. She loved being **creative**, and she noticed that her horizons expanded when she looked at life with more creativity. She wanted to **trust** experience more, but it felt too hard to find much she believes. She knew God existed, but never considered Him much. She toyed with her relationship with **faith**, and noticed it when she studied His promises; she felt more **courage** to be whom He designed her to be. She was **curious** and craved the **freedom** to **explore** her thoughts and go as she felt directed. She valued **intimacy** with like-minded people and loved when meaningful **friendships** evolved. She wanted **fun** in her life.

Tina was most excited by her **possibilities**. When her value of possibilities was partnered with her creative thoughts, more things felt adventurous and full of motivating challenges. She loved feeling herself **grow** and felt more **powerful** as a result. She loved how her life was unfolding just by leading with and considering more, her values,

Tina's **results**, in a general kind of way, began to feel more **meaningful**. The direction she was going, and the paths she chose better matched her **essence**.

These are some of the key values Tina wanted in her life because they made her feel **happy** and **motivated**. Not all of these values could be present all of the time; or at the same time, but Tina felt joyous and hopeful when as many of them as possible, were present. Before committing herself to anything or anyone, she tried to determine which of these values she thought would be present, possible, or not. She knew her standards for engagement and was comfortable asking better, at times even risky, questions to ensure she'd feel motivated. If her values were enabled, she engaged and produced personally satisfying results. When her personal values were not present, her energy was lower, inevitably in those situations, her satisfaction and results were only okay.

Tina, like many of us, assumed decisions were made for safety or security. She didn't know what else she could aspire for, or what **inspiring** results to pursue. Her lack of self-awareness kept her focused only on what she had studied and been taught. Tina, like many of us, never learned about the power of her values as it related to her real identity.

Tina expressed that her effectiveness, satisfaction, success, sexiness, and influence all increased when she began leading with and incorporating her own, God assigned values. It wasn't easy at first because she was so used to doing things to please others. Tina hadn't been out of school very long, she wanted a job, but decided to be more **selective** about her criterion for employment. She knew that some of her friends were in well-paying jobs already, but she also knew they were not **happy**. Her transformation was related to self-direction, even though that meant more part-time jobs.

Focus on that which you can control. Consider learning His promises, they are for all of us, and especially comforting when we feel alone.

Focus on increasing your self-understanding. God is good and He alone knows the fullness of our potential. He'll get us to where we are going if we let Him. Remember,

> *"In their hearts, humans plan their course, but the LORD establishes their steps." Proverbs 16:9 (NIV)*

Chapter 8

In the World but not of the World

Don't allow the world to make you think you are less than the Queen you are. You are a goddess, a daughter of God, and made in His likeness. Learn your values and then focus on them. You are better than your current reality, and your values are your road map to all the abundance you have been waiting for and promised.

He knew I would have my #MeToo story. He knew it would shut me down and harm my kids and me financially. Neither God, nor my profile spared me from personal and professional damage, but my Faith in Him, together with faith in myself, helped me stay standing. Thoughtful sophistication will empower you too, stay standing when life doesn't feel so easy!

Let's consider the world's rules for engagement. The world loves information and knowledge. Do your part, get more information and knowledge about your abilities and effectiveness. What we learn in school is even more useful when partnered with personal education, especially for those who are choosing professions that will require them to develop their clientele. Professionals who want to be independents in Law, Psychology, Business, Medicine, even clergy, to name a few, will be engaging in various forms of sales for business development and prospecting. Understand, how to make your life choices easier. It's possible with awareness! www.mapforward.org/success.

Obviously, thoughtful sophistication is possible to have without the use of technology to tell us who we've always been. Having objective, scientifically validated output, however, is information and knowledge that helps shorten the time it takes to develop our business and gets us where we want to be faster, and sooner. It is helpful information to have when considering business partnerships, entrepreneurial ventures, and even relationship compatibility! Contrary to popular belief, we don't have to learn everything about life through trial and error. We are meant to be thoughtfully sophisticated, and with this awareness, we make better more strategic choices for our lives. Some of us need to see our potential without the influence of our upbringing, negative self-talk, or surroundings. Give yourself a fresh perspective to consider yourself with, by doing so, you too. will increase your options and refine your personality!

The higher your dreams, aspirations, and vision for your life, the deeper your understanding must be of your strengths and limitations, and of the values that put a spring in your step.

Chapter 9

Developing a Vision

ronically, the concept of "Focus" is a broad topic, it acts as the gateway to all thinking: perception, learning, reasoning, problem-solving, and decision making, and includes the topic of "vision." As we've journeyed through the sections of Self-Awareness, and Focus, and as we head into the Strategy Section, hopefully, you are re-evaluating the old vision of what life should be—based on expectations—and see anew what life could be when your choices reflect your values.

Visions, like values, are personal and are experienced internally. They're the mental pictures you have of something as if it already exists, even if and when the conditions necessary for it do not, as of yet, exist. That is amongst the reasons why your visions, like your values, are beautiful; they come from within you and as such are worthy of acceptance! Your visions enhance your key values, and your key values enhance your visions. Focus on these two elements of "success" and soon enough, you'll be claiming your Throne.

Your Vision is for Change

Visions are a portrait of possibilities, and as such, they're always about change. Visions will never be about things as they are or more of the same; they're about going further than you've ever gone, extending reality beyond what you've already known. Visions are always about a better future; taking the invisible and making it visible.

You already know it's an act of courage to live by your personal values, just like you already know that not all values are equal—live whichever values that make you feel whole and present in body, mind, and soul—and lead you to your vision!

Shanti told her boss she was going to resign; she gave a multitude of legitimate reasons for her decision. Rather than accept the resignation of a value-add employee, her manager addressed each of her concerns and committed to change. Shanti was elated! She had boldly communicated what she would no longer accept and prepared to walk away from the paycheque she loved receiving. Instead, her courage and conviction were rewarded, and every aspect of her job improved, as a result.

Progress and positive change are always the outgrowths of some kind of dissatisfaction. Therefore, embrace your dissatisfaction, it leads to progress and positive change! Dissatisfaction awakens much of what has been lying dormant within us, enabling us to cross that invisible "dissatisfaction line," that divides the world: Those who choose progress, and positive change in their lives; and those who don't.

We know that one side of this line is overcrowded. It's populated by those who are threatened by their own, or others' feelings of disapproval. Courage is required to change reality. Most on this side of the line doubt, they have the courage. On the other side of the line, where I imagine you are, are those who acknowledge their restlessness and direct their focus to the possibility of change. And then, to create the kind of change their visions point them to. Accept your visions; trust the path toward change will become clearer as you go.

As T.E. Lawrence put it, *"All people dream, but not equally. Those who dream by night in the dusty recesses of their minds wake in the day to find that it was vanity; but the dreamers of the day are dangerous people for they may act their dream, with open eyes to make it possible."*

Vision and Leadership

Meaningful change comes only when people are willing to take risks. That's why leadership and vision go hand-in-hand. All leaders out there, be they of a company, country, business, community, or family, are to be intentional about sharing their rich vision. It's up to all of us to communicate our visions to the visionless so they can join us and then achieve their vision.

When Visions Are Most Powerful

Your visions are relevant and worth understanding. Your soul is trying to get your attention and show you what is possible. Visions don't force themselves on us, they are there for your consideration though. They could remain just as possibilities; among the sea of thoughts you have. However, talk about a missed opportunity! Your vision has the potential to change your life! *Your soul knows things you don't know.* Stay open to your visions! Though they are intangible and may even seem flaky if you've chosen "perfect will" for your life, pay closer attention to the visions being communicated to you. In the absence of other power inducing options, what better choice can you come up with?

Vision is enough. Your vision will nudge you forward, show you the steps to take; use your values, personality, and mindset, everything that makes you, you. It all comes from the same Source. Do the math: You are set up to be successful!

You can do anything, you don't have to struggle, and life doesn't have to be hard. It's the opposite. The more you know about yourself, the less you struggle and the more time you have to be successful. We don't have to know the steps to take, all we have to know is to not let go of the vision. You'll be haunted if you do. Letting go of vision is the genesis of regret.

As we move into the Strategy Section of the formula, remember:

Our feelings either empower us or set us up for failure if we fail to heed their warning. Develop your vision with strategies that account for the feelings which motivate you, regardless of your objectives. Identify the demotivating feelings in any situation, try to understand them, and once you do, drop whatever and whomever it is, faster than a hot potato. Move on to only energizing values, situations, and people that contribute to your unfolding abundance.

It is more than possible to have a transformation in your life, and in fact, it is probable when you reframe your perspective of the situation and find new, different, empowering possibilities and opportunities. Recruit more faith into your life; believe, trust, and know that your setbacks, challenges, and disappointment will be ultimately to your advantage.

"Oh, the places you'll go…I'm afraid that sometimes you'll play lonely games too. Games you can't win "cause you'll play against you…. But on you will go…though your arms may get sore and your sneakers may leak…I know you'll hike far and face up to your problems whatever they are." —Dr. Seuss, *Oh, the Places You'll Go!*

Still, wait for it with certainty, anyway.

Focus on trusting whom God designed you to be, move towards your vision with the values you were assigned. Lead with faith, and you will never sink. God assures those who wait on Him expectantly, that there is no risk when we focus on being the person, He designed us to be. The only risk is that we don't.

> *"Before I formed you in the womb, I knew you, and before you were born, I consecrated you; I appointed you a prophet to the nations." Jeremiah 1:5 (ESV)*

PART 3
Strategy

Self-Awareness
+ Focus
+ **Strategy**
= SUCCESS

Chapter 10

The Strategy of All Strategies

A quick recap:

Part 1—*Self-awareness*, is our most powerful tool. The intent of this section is to convey that thoughtful sophistication is all-encompassing, and why: I hope you recognize and agree that it impacts EVERYTHING.

Part 2—*Focus*, to illustrate how feelings, which are our values, have been given to us to ensure we make life-affirming choices.

Please understand that, together, our thoughtful sophistication and values, exist and come together in order to net us the most rewarding professional and personal results we are courageous enough to seek. Now we come to the strategy part of the formula.

Strategy is the pivot point between *self-awareness* and *focus*. Looked at from the shadow of our visions, strategy, is what gets us to the end goal of the formula: *Success and Sexiness*.

The Strategy of All Strategies

There are, at least, three broad strategy types. The Business strategy, which concerns itself primarily around the "how" a company will approach its opportunities. There is an Operational strategy, which is primarily concerned with questions related to capability needs and processes. And the third strategy, the Transformational strategy. While it is not as common as the other two strategies, it addresses the same issues as a business or operational strategy, and so much more!

Transformational strategies tend to be for wholesale transformation. Transformational strategies exist to cause disruptive, positive changes. Harvard Business School professor, Clayton M Christensen coined the phrase "disruptive innovation." Loosely, he applied the word "disruptive" for any "product" that enters the market in raw form and then steadily works its way up, disrupting established norms, along the way. This is the Transformational strategy, we focus on: "You," as the product, evolving from caterpillar to butterfly with the aid of thoughtful sophistication. Your ascension to your Throne, as a Queen, is disruptive to the established norms your life has followed. That is why it is a process that requires, diligence, and vigilance.

Strategy Matters

There will always be people, situations, challenges, and disappointment that slow us women down, and it is always in our best interest to know how to respond and recover, when and if, that happens. We all need a strategy, a system, that we look to, fall back on when, and if, we get delayed or blocked. With a strategy, it is easier to problem-solve. Strategies can always be re-visited and revised. Following a strategy makes trouble-shooting easier to identify where we may have tripped up, or what we may have failed to consider or incorporate, and not get delayed or blocked, in future efforts. There may be times you recognize you got in the way of your own transformation: maybe behaviors related to your personality traits were not accounted for, or maybe key motivating values were omitted. Having a strategy is efficient and strategic. In the absence of a strategy, too much time is wasted on trying to figure out how things went amiss. A strategy is something we take time to develop when we have a compelling, motivating "why." Otherwise, it is more likely we wing it. While that may feel like the easiest approach at the time, it is actually a strategy for compromise and mediocrity. There is no room for mediocrity in your transformation, the Queen you are needs her energy and confidence; mediocrity is an energy sucker.

Currently, how satisfied, on a scale of 1–10, 10 being high, are you, with how well you consciously direct and control your transformation? Whatever number you choose between 1–10, is perfect, because that is information you can use and act on. All that matters, for each and every objective you have and strategy you choose, is that you are enabled to be full-on you! Failing to plan, is planning to fail. Your strategy for transformation requires "focus" on the visions, hopes, and dreams planted inside of you: Think Big!

Look Closer

Let's presume this book got into your hands because you are ready for Transformation. If you are serious and committed to your success and sexiness, and haven't already, begin challenging some of your existing paradigms and examining more of the processes you subscribe to. Determine, IF, your approaches actually serve you to move forward. Without an examination of your current approaches, it's possible that your current approaches perpetuate what keeps you standing still, stuck; not moving forwards or backwards, just stagnating, or going round and round in circles with the same challenges, same situations, same people. Remind yourself, your focus is on your success, sexiness, and transformation. Your best results will always be a function of your thoughtful sophistication and your values.

"... With your head full of brains and your shoes full of feet, you're too smart to go down any not-so-good street." —Dr. Seuss, *Oh, the Places You'll Go!*

With your face to the sun and the wind at your back: Take a chance on you. Be the choreographer of your own dance.

"... You're on your own. And you know what you know. And YOU are the guy who'll decide where to go." —Dr. Seuss, *Oh, the Places You'll Go!*

More women are choosing to be entrepreneurial these days, the idea of hopping on and staying on a corporate bandwagon, despite the steady paycheck and benefits, holds little appeal. Women all over the world are standing up and demanding their freedom, to be. It's as though women are listening more to their Spirit and wondering what "more" there is for them. Few of us have been taught to strategize for our visions, and that's okay because now you are!

Resist the gravitational pull of your two critics as you implement some kind of strategy.

Chapter 11

Realities

Your Inner Critic

Your inner critic is the self-appointed judge who loves the status quo, whether or not, it is a favorable one. You may have already felt your inner critic trying to pull you down. It rears its ugly head any time you consider new, exciting, excellent opportunities. It's that negative voice in our head that tells us, "You're not good enough," or "You're not pretty enough," or "No one likes you." The goal of the inner critic is to keep you down, and sometimes the vicious voice in your head is a wicked force. Be prepared for this resistance from within. Stand strong. Giving the inner critic a name has made it easier for clients to push back on it in order to stay the course. For example, remember someone who has held you back in the past, and when you notice your inner critic trying to hold you back address it with the same name as the person who held you back in the past. Or, name it in whatever way that enables you to silence it. Or you can just choose to refer to it as the Gremlin. Is your gremlin working overtime right now? It's especially during difficult times when the gremlin sounds so convincing, ruins fun moments, and sabotages us from experiencing joyful ones. The good news is: You can silence your gremlin!

Your Outer Critics

Then there are the outer critics, the haters, that heave into view. It could be members of your own family, colleagues at work, or even friends—there will be no shortage of outer critics—so be prepared, and do not give in to them!

It's not out of maliciousness that these outer critics exist. Make effort to understand their "need" to make your pursuits seem unrealistic. You have changed lanes, and for you, good is no longer enough. While the opportunity is available to all of us, few actually choose to do as you're doing and fix their eyes on great. Your courage is a reminder to them of how safe they're playing.

Regardless of who we are, our DNA is programmed for growth and progress: It is right to want more! History is paved with examples of those who've done like you are doing. These individuals were rewarded with accomplishments, amassed wealth, progress, or other benefits for themselves and others, just by forging their own paths. Generally, we view such individuals as special, smarter, and luckier than us, and with more going for them, to begin with. Except, now, you too know that most special, smart and seemingly lucky individuals had a vision, and thoughtful sophistication, just like you!

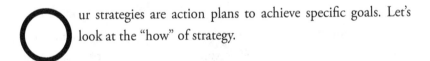

Chapter 12

Strategy is About the How

What do you want to achieve or avoid? The answers to this question are objectives. How will you go about achieving your desired results? The answer to this you can call strategy—William E. Rothschild.

Our strategies are action plans to achieve specific goals. Let's look at the "how" of strategy.

Planning

As obvious as it sounds, strategies require planning. You've taken the time to look at what's possible for you personally and, or professionally. Now ask yourself: What next? The more strategically you plan, (clear on the objective you are after, giving thought to the challenges you could face, identifying how you plan on using your personality and which values you will lead with), the better poised you'll be for your specific opportunities.

Mind Your Focus

It's a strategic error in any game—from Uno to Chess to life—to focus on the challenges or the opponents. Be aware of them, but don't focus on them, otherwise, we may feel overwhelmed, intimated, outmatched. Basically, it's too easy to give up, lose confidence, waver, react, or settle. Optimal outcomes are most assured with informed strategies and focused commitment.

Success is the natural reward for following proven processes. Your visions for success, your values, and your personality are enough. As you begin to account for and continue to factor in your unique self, your transformation begins! Use *K.I.S.S.* as your guide to focus on your unique, excellent essence, successful transformation, and personal mastery. We don't have to be rocket scientists or "famous" in order to achieve and make things happen. Every famous and successful individual started out just like you, with a desired vision they focused on and committed to. Life is not always fair, and we may feel beaten before we even get started because of all the lack we are most aware of, but get your ladder on another wall and reframe your reality. While others may have it easier in ways you may not, you have a unique, powerful, and sustainable competitive advantage; your essence! You are moving closer to being amongst an elite group of individuals who have self-awareness/thoughtful sophistication/personal mastery and those individuals are successful. Vigilantly control your unfolding.

Remember, Start from the Inside Out

Develop your strategy with concrete knowledge of who you are, and what, in your current approach, you are satisfied and pleased with. You know best and you will always be your most strategic advantage and competitive edge. Success in life is a result of becoming what you want to be, and living life on your terms as a child of God.

The goal is Transformation, a wholesale goal for your life. Just as the hip bone is connected to the knee bone: **Who you are impacts EVERYTHING!**

What area of your life will you begin with? Maybe the well-known, Wheel of Life, will help you identify areas of your life focus your energy if you don't already know.

Chapter 13

Wheel of Life Exercise

I n the 1960s, Paul J. Meyer founder of the Success Motivation Institute, divided life into eight categories, that impact, and influence, directly or indirectly, how we feel:

Physical Surroundings (physical dwellings, office space, geography, things around you)

Friends & Family (can be separated to be 2 different categories on your wheel)

Fun & Recreation

Health & Fitness

Romance

Career

Personal Growth

Money

It is natural to want to complete this exercise based on your level of active engagement in each category; don't do it that way. The exercise is for you to evaluate through the lens of satisfaction, how you feel about your life. Use the life-enhancing values you've identified for yourself when evaluating each area of the wheel, rate your satisfaction with each category. Give yourself a number for each category of the Wheel of Life, between 1-10. Work from the inside of the wheel to the outside, with one being low and closer to the center, ten at the outside of the wheel.

Upon completion of the exercise, connect the dots. Notice how closely the connected dots resemble a wheel. Is your "wheel" round, tight or bumpy? How would you feel if one of the wheels on the cars your travel in resembled your Wheel of Life? Imagine the ride if it was a wheel on the car you are in. Except, it is much more important than even a wheel of a car; it's your life, a visual of the life you are currently living. Is your ride as smooth as you'd like it to be?

Feeling the Energy

All areas within the Wheel of Life matter and affect us but to varying degrees. Focus on the areas of your life you feel pulled towards or energy for. Be sure you rate your satisfaction score being guided by your feelings (values), how present your "must-have" values are. Different categories pull us at different times, and this is true throughout the various seasons of our life. Keep the focus on energy at this season of your life. If your energy directs you to improve your score/satisfaction with money, easy peasy, within your potential is a pot of gold. Work backwards, with a clear awareness of what you want; apply what you've known, and have learned about yourself.

1. the strengths of your personality,
2. the feelings you want more of in your life, and
3. acknowledge some of the persistent visions you have.

Upon completion of these very important steps in your journal, pray, for guidance to ensure you succeed. Focus on living the life you desire. Manifest your paths by keeping a single-minded focus on the vision. The wheel exercise is useful to do at any time; whether you are feeling restless, or because you sense it is time for a re-do, there is intel each time the exercise is completed. Question no more; You have everything it takes to realize whatever goal you want if you truly want it. Commit to memory this truth; when we flow with the direction of our energy, and opportunities, WE SUCCEED, and it is your time. If you have trouble finding the developmental opportunities to lead you to transformation, call me. I'm happy to help, please reach out AFTER you have taken the time to identify your success triggers.

Your thoughtful sophistication will guide you to your Throne!

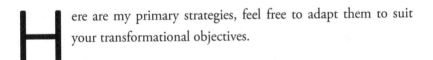

Chapter 14

Strategies

H ere are my primary strategies, feel free to adapt them to suit your transformational objectives.

The Get Rich Strategy

We all, quite naturally, want to become all that we are capable of becoming. In order to realize this potential, we are required to be all that we can be. This strategy, though I call it the "Get Rich Strategy," is about being successful, in the ways that you want to be. The strategy borrows from *The Science of Getting Rich*, a classic, written by *Wallace D. Wattles published in 1910 by the Elizabeth Towne Company.*

In order to live, and feel the completeness of a satisfying life, a great amount of wealth is required. There is nothing wrong with wanting to be rich and there is nothing wrong with being rich! In essence, when a woman desires to be rich, what she is really doing is claiming her readiness to live a fuller and more abundant life. How can that be wrong? It is a known fact that the object of life is progress, evolution, and development; to that end, we are each required to develop to the maximum of our abilities. You are entitled and expected to want all that Nature freely gives, whether that is elegance, beauty, or the freedom to do as you choose. It is all available to you and exists for your betterment; progress and evolution. Getting rich, like any pursuit we long for, is a function of your mindset and strategy. Getting rich is not only for those with some kind of natural ability; think of all the unintelligent, untalented, and unattractive people that get rich. You don't have to be very intelligent, or gifted, or creative, or attractive, or meaning-seeking, or, or, or.

You have to get really clear on how badly you want to be rich. Then, develop that focused mindset. Know the key personal values you have that could, in some way, enable you to be rich. Give thought as to what being rich will advance. Embrace the mindset of abundance. You have the ability to be rich, we all do!

For us to develop into our best, we must have access to all the things that will strengthen us in body, mind, and soul. The easiest most direct way to attain what is needed is by obtaining wealth. Therefore, develop a strategy to increase your income. Commit to and notice the values that are involved in each step. Some of the values have been underlined for you, but a few may have been missed.

1. You have innate possibilities and the sole purpose of nature is to advance and develop life through each of us. Using your thoughtful sophistication, how do you define and measure "success." Then,

2. Measure your success by becoming all you want to be and having all that you want to have. If you want to bake pies, be a mission-

ary or a tycoon; having money advances objectives faster, giving you time to enjoy the fruits of your labor, sooner.

But money isn't actually the goal to focus on. *The focus is to be on delivering quality results* (value), now. Your ability to do so is what generates money: Focus on being good at what you do, and the money to live a richer, fuller life of abundance, will follow.

The woman who tells herself that she doesn't have any abilities to deliver quality results and get rich is wrong. The woman who tells herself she doesn't desire to live more abundantly cannot realize her potential. The woman who does not want to have the money needed to buy what she really wants is not being honest with herself.

To have a fulfilling, abundant life, you are required to realize your full potential. None of us has ever seen or can imagine, what the future has in store for those who develop their potential. Remember, your purpose is to claim your Throne as the Queen of You!

You have been given desires to be realized and values by which they can be realized!

We are to use our hands to build, to play instruments, to paint beautiful pictures—and, get rich doing so.

We are to use our eyes to see all the beauty around us and contribute to its ongoing development(value), and get rich,

We are to use our voices for truth(value) and to sing(value) beautiful songs and get rich, doing so.

Money is needed to advance. Commit to understanding, and incorporating, your thoughtful sophistication and approach everything, with it. If you do, those who want to use their hands and need instruments and tools to use, in order to develop their talents fully, and enhance life around them, will have them. Those who appreciate beauty will find themselves surrounded by beautiful things. Those who appreciate clothes will be beautifully clothed. Both will do beautiful things for others.

Foodies can be assured they will be fed only the finest and will have businesses that enable them to share their gifts with others. We are to have all the things that we are capable of appreciating, doing, and having. We are to use the gifts we've been given to make the world better. Our only requirement is to mentally focus and take informed, intentional actions.

Laws of the Universe are available for anyone to use, the clearer you are on your objectives, the more useful these laws will be to you, in your strategy. These laws can be applied to anything, when followed, they assure you, as you are, where you are, that you are very able to become wealthy, or whatever else it is, you most want.

Your time is now, and your best days are ahead of you. Use your thoughtful sophistication.

These spiritual laws, when studied, enable you to develop a more precise, better picture of your place in the world. With an understanding of these laws, you can get rich!

We already know that obstacles occur, and sometimes these obstacles leave us feeling lost and confused about our purpose. We may even feel like no amount of planning or strategizing makes a difference. Except, that is not true. Look at the different laws, study them, trust them. They harness truths that provide perspective. Be sure to lead with influencing variables like faith, hope, and love and ensure your actions have focused passion for the results you are capable of achieving.

1. Be clear about "why" you want to obtain wealth.

    When you know and lead with a compelling "why"; naturally, your more intentional about finding and attracting those things, people, and opportunities that resonate with your values. You'll earn more by being your best. Those things, people, and opportunities with whom you and your values resonate will recognize you and help you.

    Yes, money makes it possible to realize more of the world, but don't focus on loving money. Love the "feelings" and abilities having money elicits. A primary principal in The Science of Getting Rich is to always give five times more in "use value" than you receive in "cash value" for your products or services.

2. Focusing on your excellence is enough to achieve wealth.

Why not, the Universe is friendly to your desires. You've got everything you need, even if you think you lack talent, ability, or intellect. It's not about being perfect, or in the right business industry, place, or company, at the right time that determines your destiny.

What matters is that you do what you enjoy doing, and you do it well because that attracts more opportunities, more people, more things, and more money to you. The sooner you focus on attracting opportunity, people, things to you, the sooner you get rich. Even if you are broke, it will come, your best is still ahead of you. Even if you have no real support, no real safety net of a partner, friends, or family, your best is still ahead of you. It doesn't even matter if you don't have the capital you've determined you need. With faith, application, and remembrance of these truths, you will be led to your destiny, or it will be brought to you. Focus clearly on where you are headed, keep praying, and be grateful, it is all there, just waiting for you to claim it. It is that simple, and you have everything it takes. Your best days are ahead of you.

While God is the cornerstone of every part of what I encourage. That is not to say, in the spirit of free will, you can't do it without Him. Just know that when we try to do anything without Him, we lose the perfect guidance that only He can give, and usually end up feeling empty for it. But you get to choose a permissive strategy or a perfect one.

God wants us all, including you, to have all that is deemed good. He wants you to be all that you are capable of being and having all that you are capable of having. He doesn't want any of us to lack in anything. Evolution is our destiny, and Nature seeks growth. Therefore, when we evolve, we advance, grow, and move forward. The world is a big place and we can't even fathom the opportunities and possibilities that exist! We all have the opportunity to engage more actively with the evolution of life. We all want to live more; life wants us all, to live more.

Keep your eyes focused on your excellence.

3. You already have everything you need to advance your objectives. You can have what you dare to want.

Get clear on your strengths, values, and blind spots.

Focus your thoughts on your desires, daily. The more you focus on them, and apply your strengths and values, the sooner they will come.

4. Focus on the truth of your values. It takes effort and energy but pays enormous dividends.

Life was intended to be blissful. Stay focused on what you want to be manifested for you.

When we live in flow with our values, truth and opportunity come to us.

Your reality is that you are destined for abundance. Hold tightly to that truth. Look for its presence everywhere; grow into your potential.

We are to increase, expand, and grow, that is the privilege of living. To be satisfied with "good," or "enough," actually stunts the evolutionary process.

We make the world a better place by making ourselves better, first, then getting rich.

Learn more about yourself so you can fill your space and move on to a bigger one—rich!

You deserve your destiny. Be assured that what you desire, is truly possible for you!

Realize the more you desire "it," the more you can be assured that it is possible for you.

Give all your unexpressed desires a chance to be realized.

Trust yourself. Live more, have more, and be more.

Do not allow anyone to suggest that a healthy desire for wealth is greed; it is a desire for life.

5. Want riches AND do your part: Be the best you possible.

Make the most of yourself for yourself and others. With desire and faith Girlfriend, you are unstoppable. Thank God daily that it is so.

Develop a mindset of gratitude.

To not do so reduces the likeliness that His blessings will always be so abundant.

We know setbacks happen, in order to obtain abundance, if that is our strategy, then our focus has to be on getting rich; not our setbacks. The more we talk about our bad breaks, our challenges, and our lack, the more we delay our riches.

If you have accepted the two premises made at the beginning of this strategy that: God has given you inherent possibilities: and, the sole purpose of nature is to advance and develop life, focus and advance these two truths.

For this strategy to work, all of your focus has to be on achieving abundance: directly, consistently. Only focus on increasing your income streams. Give no thought to what others say, be still, and wait. Literally. Get organized, minimize your expenses, and cover your bill, daily give thanks, and focus on the abundance that is waiting for you.

Every one of us has the right to be on this path. There is enough for all of us. To not have ensured enough for all of us would make God cruel. God is only loving. There is enough to go around.

Let us use our knowledge, attitude, and compassion to inspire those who don't already know that they too can realize their potential and obtain wealth.

All any of us has to do is focus our strategy on a vision for success.

Always take the high road, focus on your vision, and never lose hope. Doors will open and paths you never thought possible will be cleared for you. All you have to do is increase your self-awareness, understand the power in your values, and develop a clear vision. I encourage you to include God in your strategy, let Him do His part.

6. Use your ability to think; it gives you the power to create.
    This ability is self-evident because before you begin anything you think about the result, you intend to produce. Be clear about what you want to create for yourself or for others.

7. Get started today. Do all you can do where you are now.
    Be ready to advance and fill the spaces where you currently exist. You want to progress, and you are ready.

    Start where you are. Before you can be advanced evolution requires you to fill your existing spaces. All that means is you be more present, focused, and engaged, now, to be rich later.

    As for those areas in our lives that don't inspire us enough to care; when we knowingly leave things undone, we create unnecessary and avoidable delays. Let's not.

    Do everything you can to fulfill each responsibility you have, well. If there is too much on your plate, find a creative way to remove activities not contributing to your generation of wealth. Non-advancing opportunities delay more than just the realization of riches; inadvertently they also contribute to the delay of evolution and progress. Nothing and no-one can advance unless the space allotted to them is filled. Disengagement is understandable. However, to not address the issue and instead tolerate mediocrity from ourselves delays us from moving forward as we have not filled the space nature has allotted us. The more we accept being less than we are, live with less than we want, the sooner we find ourselves in realities we despise.

If you have to do it, do it well so you can stop having to do what you despise. You control the pace by which you advance.

Fill the places where you are if you want to have progress in your life. Be the best woman you can be, as a mom, wife, daughter, sister, employee, friend, partner, renter, or homeowner. Even if it feels thankless, fill your space so you can outgrow it and move on.

Fill your place, not to please others or receive recognition, but so you can advance yourself. Some days it will be easier to do than others.

The objective is to have more successful days than not. Be your best as often as you are willing, doing so will bring you all the riches the Universe has waiting for you!

Your destiny is waiting for you to engage more with your life so you can be rich.

8. Remember, even though we can't always know how we're influencing our results, even the little things matter.

The forces in the universe have been put into motion working with us, for us, and on our behalf.

Inconsistency delays our progress. We don't know which of the actions we take will open our doors to opportunity and great possibilities. Let's not tolerate any more delays. Don't become crazy intense about it and think it all has to be done now. Just do the things of your day well.

The more days you do well the sooner you live a successful life.

Use your mind to work out your visions and reality. Even if you are thinking to yourself, "I've no energy left to keep pushing," remember:

9. You're not alone to realize your results.
   Success is your destiny.

10. Control your mental energy with faith
    It is crazy comforting to know that in times of challenges we can be still; it's okay to do nothing!

    We are not to hurry or rush or try to force anything. By doing nothing in the actual, we are enabled to be more creative mentally, as we wait patiently in faith. There are no shortages of opportunity, even if "this one" seems impressive. If it passes, let it go, that means an even more amazing one is en route.

    Wait for it, enable your "miracles."

    Put all your faith and purpose into your efforts mentally and advance your objectives by fully filling the spaces you are in right now.

    Do it this way and do not waiver: You will indeed get rich.

    This is not about wanting and wishing, that approach too often ends in frustration and disappointment.

    Consistent and faithful mental action towards a clear vision produces results and brings all the forces of the universe to your service. Your faith will be rewarded. Be patient.

11. Strong faith but half-baked efforts suggest uncertainty about your conviction. Just like great efforts with no faith, offer no real peace, sustainable results, conviction, or satisfaction.
    It is better to do nothing as long as you do it with faith than it is to keep trying and wasting your energy and morale. Faith is not an easy thing to lead with, though, and the only way to maintain it is by drawing closer to God, so you can understand His promises.

When you take actions depending on God, success will be realized. The more success you have with doing and being your best every day, the more other achievements will follow

12. Success is cumulative.
The more we move forward, evolve, and realize more of our potential, the more things people and opportunities will attach to you.

13. The desire for growth and progress is inherent in all things.
The faster you want to realize your clear vision, the more you must focus on it with faith.

Be obsessively focused on be faithful, doing things in this way enables the picture of what you want, to get clearer and more precise. Soon, it will be always at the forefront of your mind.

Continue filling your existing spaces well and notice how your enthusiasm for life grows. Your overall energy level will increase. Protect it. Maintain it.

You can certainly do what you want to do. Your sustained desire for a vision is proof that you have the power to realize that which you desire.

There is power in desire.

14. Offer increase, of any kind, to those around you.
Knowing we all must increase, and we all have something that offers increase to others, naturally attracts, and draws others to us.

Look at the values that most inspire you, within those values, is the gift of increase you have to offer others.

When you understand and believe in your ability to offer an increase, you can communicate it to others, and they will seek you out.

With faith and purpose, you have every ability to get rich.

It is easy to find money-making options via endless searching on the Internet.

It is right to want and have an increase in life.

15. Form a clear mental picture of your vision, use your self-awareness, incorporate your values, apply your faith and purpose to it.

With determination, comes advancement. Others will feel your power of purpose. They will sense you have changed and are advancing and will also be inspired to pursue increase.

16. Opportunity will find you.

Don't worry yourself if others seem to be advancing faster or more than you. Your objectives and results may require more faith and patience. That's okay, remember the higher the building, the deeper must be the foundation.

17. In the interim, look for ways you can help those around you who want to advance.

Doing so actually advances you too. When we grow and help others to grow, we help God.

18. You don't have to wait for the perfect opportunity

When an opportunity to be more, now, is presented and you feel drawn to it, take it. Greater opportunities will follow.

19. Nothing and no one can hold you down unless on some level you don't think you can advance or don't want more for your life.

20. If you want more, and dream with faith in your clear vision, it is possible for you, nothing, and no-one can stop you.

21. Always, and only, think and speak in terms of your advancement.

All kinds of people and things delay women. But, nothing and no one can keep a woman down.

You are blessed with the ability to create what you want.

With faith, everything is possible.

As you can see, each actionable is directed to reframing your mindset, while focusing on your essence. Your fortune lies in your essence.

Look for hope and purpose for your life, it is inside you, and you will find it. If you can't see it, call me: 905–582–6030, and, or, sign up for the 4-week online course, "Self-Awareness for Success." The latter option will help you more than just a 15-minute chat with me. Of course, you can avail yourself of both options. All that matters is you understand yourself enough to engage your values. The active presence of your must-have values will ensure your successful evolution. Everything, our successes, and failures will, and continue to be influenced by our strengths, values, and blind spots. The Get Rich strategy, if you incorporate the above directives and controllables, will render you Rich.

It's a journey. Sometimes, we'll be more successful than others, and sometimes opportunities may not play out as we hoped, that's okay. We get re-do's and we can lead with more personal mastery in our next attempt.

The Results Strategy

Results orientation is about the desire for results. This value is inside all of us. Even if others do not appreciate the results, we tend to most value; they are still results. Don't get in the habit of pushing aside the results you want to be accomplished because somebody else doesn't value that same result. That's their issue. You have the courage, inner strength, and thoughtful sophistication to be able to defend and move forward. Trust yourself. Keep committing to delivering results.

Results are results. To make a gourmet dinner is to achieve a result. If you pride yourself on your excellent planning/organizing, let yourself focus on the results, an end deliverable. If you enjoy canvassing for a cause, do it and measure your effectiveness by the number of doors you knock on, or conversations you have…results. If you can achieve results anywhere, you can do it everywhere. Incidentally, each of these three results-focused activities are income streams that could be developed…

Meet Nina

Nina told me she didn't care so much about results, and then she preceded to describe the weekend that passed and told me all about the things she did and how much that thrilled her. She had researched, organized, and collectivized her group of friends' activity, and it was a hit! Nina did not acknowledge how results-focused she had been to make it all happen. She loved doing the preparatory pieces to enable the outing; the excursion, the result, but to her, the result was just the by-product. It took her a while to recognize how often in her life she judges the concept of being results-focused and gets put off too quickly when she is asked to deliver on results at work. She began reframing more of her activities, she had just developed a blind spot relative to results. In her role as assistant manager, she learned to look more objectively and looked for values, she could leverage. As a result, she was more motivated and delivered better results.

It seems obvious, almost simplistic, I agree, but that's the point! God never designed life to be hard or a struggle. We reject the simplicity of that truth because we are led to believe that it has to be hard, and we have to struggle, "no pain, no gain." When we play to our values, there is no pain, only gain.

You have been hardwired to thrive, not just survive! Decide where in your life you want transformation and then develop a strategy that leverages your best, and make it happen! Only put your metaphorical ladder against the "walls" that appeal to you. You may think, "Yeah, but

I don't have that luxury to do as I want; I have bills to pay..." Many roads can get us to our destination, and provide the needed money for bills. You alone get to decide the path you will choose to get there. You can choose to be inspired and engaged as you get money to cover the bills, or you can choose to work, just for the paycheck. Choose the road that will move forward feeling inspired; you will get your paycheck and so much more. Be more conscious of putting aside a few dollars each paycheque now, so you don't feel so stressed, if the inspirational opportunity you are waiting for takes longer, set yourself up so you can wait for the result you are after. Wait for it, and if you can/do, IT WILL COME. In the interim, see who/how you can help others. Money is paper, paper grows on trees, Nature/God assures us of an abundance of leaves on trees. Trust in the process of life.

The world needs results to keep progressing and evolving, just like we do; otherwise, we stagnant and then regress. Results orientation is a value. In your strategy development focus on it, even if you don't consider results orientation as an essential value to you. The ability to achieve results is a moneymaking opportunity, and garnishes respect, especially from men. Consider the results you are good at realizing and enjoy doing. Men seem to be more naturally encouraged to be results-focused; it is a carryover from the animal kingdom when it was up to them to provide for their families, while the mama bears stayed back to protect the cubs. We, women, have the opportunity to surprise, delight, and be providers too. Plus, WE have the privilege and option of creating wonderful cubs to carry the torch forward!

Focus on your results orientation more and use it more intentionally to make lots of money. The woman who can express and deliver results, whatever they may be, and make money while doing it, will fill her space and move on to even more abundance. Identify the motivating values that produce results you can charge money for, you have abilities by which you can create respectable income streams, find them.

Whether or not we like the values and personality we have to work with, there is potential hidden within each of us, identify which aspect of your potential you want to develop modify or transform.

The Sophistication Strategy

Meet Jackie

Jackie didn't like her personality profile; she was sure her personality was different than what her report stated. **She** provided the responses to the psychometric assessment, and though most do not argue with their data, Jackie did. She knows best for herself and chose to reject the results of her scientifically validated assessment. Jackie had an image of who she wanted to be and seemed to have unconsciously determined that she could change her personality, not be who she really was. I respect determination and conviction for a vision. I also know that when our values or personality style don't support our vision, life is hard, harder than it has to be. An uphill, demotivating, and mediocre, at best, journey. Jackie jumped from position to position, company to company, always blaming the role or the company for her lack of better results. My wish for her was that she could embrace herself as she was. After we accept and embrace what is, we are better poised to develop the behaviors we want. However, in times of stress, even when our behavioral adaptability is strong, we can only ever truly be the person we indeed are. It doesn't matter if you like who you are, you are who you are: we realize our best results when we embrace that truth and go with our natural flow.

In the absence of knowing our strengths, blind spots and values-sustainable success takes too long to achieve!

Lisa is a prime example of this.

Lisa was very results-focused and practical, like Jackie, she didn't love everything in her profile, but she recognized the truth of her assessment. *Rather than resist her reality, she shifted her attention to the behaviors and values that she could refine better or engage more. She was ambitious and knew that she had to do something different to obtain another level of success. Her map forward required her to regroup and re-evaluate to get from where she was to where she wanted to be. She also was able to ask herself if she wanted to try faking aspects of her style/behaviors. She reasoned that if she lived as someone other than who she naturally was, it would take more energy to maintain that façade, then she had.*

I encourage you to do just as Lisa did; use your sophistication to achieve the next level of success in your life. There will always be individuals who achieve success sooner than we do and realize their potential before us. Just as there will always be those who recognize their progress and potential after us. There will always be lesser and greater persons than ourselves. All you can do is control your standard of excellence. Embrace your potential because one size does not fit all in this big beautiful world full of possibilities and hope.

Lynn wished she had Samantha's life and profile. However, what she didn't know is that Samantha spent the first quarter of her life in a very uncomfortable reality that influenced all her responses to life: Samantha's only hope was to stay focused on generating better results for a better life one day. Lynn had a more comfortable life in that she was loved, encouraged, and supported, and as a result, she was able to focus on whatever results or values she wanted, or not! She had not taken the time to establish much clarity for herself and found herself stuck in a world where she felt at the mercy of others because she didn't have clear goals, or a vision, or awareness. She wanted to be more intentional in her life but didn't know how to. Lynn had a much "easier" and by all measurements, a "better" life than Samantha. However, Samantha developed a strong sense of herself and her possibilities because of her lack.

The Wisdom Strategy

This is a strategy specifically for when we must work with men in parallel or senior positions, effortless variables to control, which you may find useful.

1. Communicate your intentions, desires, and objectives with clarity.
2. Once clarity is achieved, track how/if things are progressing to ensure that your objectives are being met.
3. Next, what kind of support do you want/need, in order to realize your mandates.
4. When progress is not tangible, ask direct questions to know what you need to be doing more of or differently. Journal it all, including dates, or copies of emails in the case that things are not playing out as you were assured.
5. As you plan your career, make an effort to know what your blind spots could be. With awareness of them, you can manage them because they are no longer blind to you. Sometimes, it is enough to reframe your perception but sometimes, even when we do and try to account for our blind spots, our strategy just tanks.

Look at how I handled myself with the CEO of the multinational, for example. He was in an unfulfilling marriage and always-suggesting dinner rather than office meetings. I reframed the situation and told myself he was making time for me on his short business trips, out of a sincere intent to reciprocate value. I chose not to register or process the subtle remarks he made and just focused on developing my agenda for more business. I did a cost: benefit analysis but my ambition created a blind spot.

The point is to thrive in a man's world, we must remember that it's not in our best interest, to make it easy for them to abuse their power. Their animal instincts sometimes cloud their judgment. That doesn't mean we are to give up our ambitions, hope, or idealism, or that all men are this way, it just means that we must always be thinking about and tracking all tangible results including short-term, medium-term, and long term. No one likes to walk away from what they feel they've earned or deserve, but to thrive in a man's world, we can't allow our ambition to blind us. Letting our ambitions blind us sets us to be the prey and enables them to be the predator. Of course, not all men are this ruthless, realize that many are.

We are smarter than our vulnerability makes us feel. Yes, the need placed on us to be our own defenders is draining and reduces our focus from the success we are trying to achieve, but hey, forewarned, is forearmed. Although it can be exhausting, in the end, we will be victors in our own lives.

1. Assess the situations you are in better. Recognize that if you are going into any situation where there are more men or more men who hold the balance of the power, you are immediately more vulnerable simply because men are carrying more of the cards than you are, professionally.

2. Once you feel like you have a better sense of your situation, reconsider your expectations, are they realistic. Is there a better way to manage your process and journey?

Be alert

Look around you, look within, use your understanding of values to search for the values that you sense are driving those around you, and what they might be thinking. You may think you are wearing a power suit and will be taken more seriously for it, but if they are thinking "she's got nice legs," or a "nice ass," or asking themselves "are her breasts real," your audience has checked out and aren't listening to you.

Be discerning

As a female salesperson, on the one hand, it works to our advantage because we can be effective with both genders, on the other hand, it may be nothing for a male prospect to keep you engaged in the sales cycle with him, not because he has the intention of buying from you, but because he wants to increase the likelihood of you accepting his advance. Be okay walking away from "opportunities." Remember, we can't lose what we never had. New opportunities will come.

1. Reclaim your confidence
2. Communicate how the process works, establish an upfront contract with prospective clients, agree upfront that after the second meeting, the prospective client agrees to make a decision. Don't leave him wiggle room to play/disrespect you. Sometimes, even if you sense a dangerous agenda, but confident in your ability to move the needle in your favor, use your creativity, results focus, and risk tolerance and make things happen. Evolved men will always respect the mind of a woman; therefore, it is up to us to lead with our minds. Generally speaking, they aren't expecting to see this kind of strength, and you may miss the opportunity to showcase it, otherwise.
3. Lead more emphasizing your focus on results. The men you work with may not be looking for it; you must lead with it.
4. Differentiate yourself as a woman, lead with your sharp mind; do so, and the world is your oyster of pearls and more doors will open for you.
5. Learn to develop your ability to speak directly.
6. Incorporate results orientation to your list of must-have values.
7. Look for the existence of supporting values to help you push for results, i.e., "service," or "meaning," or whatever. Make sense?
8. Look for the evolved men who remember they have moms, wives, daughters, or sisters and treat women with respect.

However, if they didn't or don't like any of those women, you may secretly just be "tits and ass," and not taken seriously. Assess the landscape associated with the men you work with, because at some point; they will influence your results, know your audience.

1. Recognize the natural selfishness of humanity. We all want what we want.
2. As a woman, do not absolve yourself from responsibility for your own life.
3. It is the exception, not yet the norm, that another person will lead you to your best; most are focused on self-preservation and advancing their agenda first.
4. However, women are finally in a position to influence which aspects of humanity are to be preserved. The #MeToo era seeks to safeguard a future with more gender equality.
5. We don't have to know or understand everything, that would be impossible, ensure you know enough to feel comfortable and safe, moving forward.
6. If you can't feel that way, where you are, use your sophistication to find a better fit or different people.
7. Until you feel comfortable with your understanding of your landscape, keep your cards close to your chest.

There will be men who can and will and want to help you simply because you deserve or need it and they can, but do not lead with your wants/needs or let your wants/needs be too apparent. When we share, before, or without knowing and feeling like it is okay to do so, we increase our vulnerability.

1. Self-employed women are especially vulnerable and have no safety nets of a Human Resources department to "protect them." Therefore, reduce your vulnerability and focus on being able to "protect yourself" in the ways you can.
2. Always assess your safety level, determine if you think they like their spouse? If you sense they don't or are not appreciated by their partner, they become a risk for you.

All I encourage you to do is notice, register it in your very intuitive mind, and not forget it. We can't do it without them, but they can't do it without us, either. It is symbiotic. Everyone, men and women, understands the necessity of being more vigilant and that is a good thing for all of us!

1. Make sure you find safe men, those who you notice believe in something good. Please know that, it's okay to like numerous things about them, such as their personality, position, sense of humor. However, I urge you to be clear and honest with yourself about your objectives, so you avoid any problems for yourself. Mr. CEO was a good man, who seemed to believe in kindness, yet I got played. At the end of the day, men are men, and women are women.

2. If we notice aspects of them that won't help us realize our objectives and maybe problems later, MOVE ON fast! If that is not possible, follow the above suggestions.

3. Decide which watch outs you are okay with managing and manage them even better. You have to. Like it or not, we are vulnerable in this man's world.

4. Be on guard with those men who have "mommy issues"; they are dangerous to our wellbeing. At a deep level, not of their choosing, they may be indifferent to women's needs.

5. When we change the dance steps, men have to respond in kind.

6. Understand yourself enough to find the right niche, environment. Much of your experience will change as a result, for the better. That doesn't mean your "ah-ha" moment will translate into immediate results, whether in the quality of clients or the velocity of cash flow.

7. Be prepared to have your conviction tested; it's just part of the weeding out process for success.

8. Have faith in yourself.

9. Don't just go along to get along, because you fear that if you don't, all will be lost. Faith assures us that there will always be more opportunities.

10. Patience is key. When we are ambitious, we can be blinded and cut corners to move ourselves along faster. Remember, anything worth having requires effort, which usually means more time than we want results to take. If you have a natural sense of urgency, that's fine. Just recognize that there are more methodical ways to push forward.

11. Be clear about the results you are after. Money and position are vague objectives. What position do you want? How much money do you want?

12. Identify what could slow you down.

13. Always expect the best and be prepared for the worst. It will allow you to regroup faster.

14. Details matter; too much focus on them, or not enough, can become a blind spot to opportunity or challenge. When we think too broadly, it is easy to explain things away and think we are wise by focusing on the big picture. There is truth in that, and at the same time, the devil is hidden in those details that we dismissed, dismiss details and it is likely they will get us. Consider all that impacts your reality, more honestly.

Nothing may change after we take such precautions, but at least we won't feel so blind-sided and can know, by choice or by error, how we were part of the problem.

1. Notice if you are being seduced by the need for other's satisfaction. Those who love you will love you more for your courage to maintain hope and conviction.

2. The ones that don't or can't support you will eventually fall by the wayside, and new people will appear that support, encourage, and validate you.

We are entering a new world, and the rules are more in our favor. It is not about being different than you already are at the core; it is just about intentionally embracing who you have been designed to be. Unless we increase our confidence and have better self-care, we will be at the mercy of the situations.

Strategies are flawed when they are not steeped in awareness and understanding of how we personally deliver excellence. Our sophistication of life, our confidence level, and our values are pieces of information that will consistently impact our results and the effectiveness of our strategies.

1. For sustainable happiness, focus first from the inside out. Models and expectations change. Who we are, doesn't.

2. Develop the habit of asking for clear communication, eliminate ambiguity to the degree you can as it relates to your objectives or expectations.

3. When the progress you are expecting, wanting, or have been assured is not forthcoming, or as tangible as you'd like, ask direct questions to know what you need to be doing more of or differently. The questions will show you are alert, aware, and on top of things. You will not follow blindly. The response to your queries will tell you much about the lay of the land.

4. Document or journal everything. Even if you only record the dates when you asked specific questions or were made particular promises. Having a record of such things may prove to be useful and doesn't require much effort.

These are just some easy to integrate directives, to help you avoid your own #MeToo story. People, companies, and shareholders are forced to care lest something that was controllable blows up in their faces. The above suggestions will be useful to keep in mind; control what you can control.

While some of my points may seem inconvenient, and you may dismiss my rather direct yet not fixed, directives because you wonder if I am cynical or bitter, nope, I'm not. I love men. My son is my most favorite man in the world! I have four brothers, I had a father, my clients have been mostly men, and I was with my husband for 13 years. I have a soft spot for men. I make these suggestions because I care about "you," and wish I had been told to be more discerning. The points are simply to highlight that we must each understand and accept responsibility for our success.

The Strategy of Faith

For lots of reasons, this strategy is the most challenging and also the most reliable, results-focused one.

Knowing how to stand firm or get back up if you've been pushed down isn't always obvious. Losing hope, however, leads to feeling helpless, trapped, or stuck and the thought of developing a strategy completely uninteresting and maybe even pointless if we allow ourselves to give up.

This is a powerful strategy because you need to do nothing, per se, other than believe in who you are. The best approach when we feel helpless, trapped, stuck, or demotivated is to adopt a strategy that leaves it all up to God.

"Be still, and know that I am God." Psalm 46:10 (ESV)

This strategy is challenging because though we love the idea of being taken care of and protected, it is just not how we are taught or encouraged to live, and the easiest option is to find a sugar daddy who will do this for us, and fight our battles for us. But that is absolutely not a sustainable strategy, and you will not realize your Throne if you put your hopes in the hands of another mere mortal. You can, however, leave your hopes and Throne aspirations in the hands of God.

"Commit your way to the LORD; trust in him, and he will act." Psalm 37:5 (ESV)

Just leave it with God and trust Him to handle it. Do this just by speaking into the void, and stating, "I'm leaving this with you, God, you said if I do, you'll help me." He has to take it if we give it to Him because He said He would.

Your role in receiving that which you've asked Him for is to keep your focus on His promises. You can do that by googling for scriptures of His promises. Then, focus on your values to help you not change your mind. Then, wait expectantly for your break; it's coming. The most challenging part of this strategy is that it requires a deeper level of trust, faith, and dependence than most of us like existing with. But, if you are just tired, drained of your zest, without direction but willing and desirous of your Throne; there is no better strategy for you than the strategy of faith! Your best days are ahead of you and God knows all about it, and will get you to where you are going! He is aware of the past, present, and future. He knew we'd get stuck, feel sad and alone, and have the challenges we have. He let things play out as they have. BUT God didn't make our challenges or setbacks happen. He gave us free will, and unfortunately, as a result, sometimes good people do bad things that cause hurt and bad things happen. Though difficulties occur, and God didn't cause them; He promises they will not be in vain. He has a plan and is using those setbacks to move us forward to an even better future. Even though you can't see or know what He's up to.

> *"You intended to harm me, but God intended it all for good." Genesis 50:20 (NLT)*

Promises like these can be a lifesaver while functioning in the world. Who wants to feel alone when life is hard? He doesn't need our false bravado; He understands why and how things shut us down. He doesn't want us to feel broken and sad. He wants us to remember that He is in complete control. Your best days are ahead of you, and He is at work behind the scenes, bringing new opportunities to you even though you can't see, know or feel like He cares. Keep the faith and wait expectantly for doors to open. Your time is now, and your best days await you. Stay focused on what you want to achieve and notice how new people come into your life.

Your focused determination will inspire others to keep moving forward in courage and faith for their desires. Keep the faith and wait for it. Remember these two scriptures:

> *"Faith is confidence in what we hope for and assurance about what we do not see." Hebrews 11:1 (NIV)*

> *"For we walk by faith, not by sight." 2 Corinthians 5:7 (ESV)*

Focus on the values you can control like faith, hope, and love. You've come too far to tolerate or believe setbacks could be your fate, no way! Your destiny is abundance.

God is currently arranging the right people and the right opportunities for you. Be ready, keep your hope alive, and stand firm. Remember, God won't do what God alone can do, if you don't ask, invite, or let Him, in Jesus' name.

> *"Whatever you ask in My name, that will I do, so that the Father may be glorified in the Son. If you ask Me anything in My name, I will do it." John 14:13–14 (NASB)*

The Investment Strategy

I was once told by a millionaire client that there is no better investment to make than into yourself. Regardless of how your journey to self-discovery and success plays out, don't limit yourself. You can achieve anything you are bold enough to desire, and all that is required is you tap into any of the values that energize you and keep you focused on your bold desires and visions with hope.

Play with your design. We're Queens, with or without a King.

Moving Forward

Fortunately, we are at a time in history where all is possible. This season is your time, so I encourage you to explore your possibilities. Please make time to understand your depth and breadth. You owe yourself that.

For those of us still trying to understand how or what it means to be a woman, we are required to peel off the layers of expectation and pressure we've grown up accepting. It isn't easy, but it is doable, reframe your paradigm by focusing on how to be your best, the person you are designed to be. Both genders exist in cultures with stereotypes that typically require us to live always trying and wanting to feel like we fit in, and that we are enough. As women, we tend to also deal with feelings of inadequacy: not thin enough, not young enough, not attractive enough, our homes aren't large and spotless enough, or our children aren't well mannered and clean-faced enough, or our dreams are not orderly and profitable enough. However, that's not how success in life is truly measured. Decide for yourself what it means for you to be a woman, a mother, and a success.

You are perfect. You are worthy. Success, however, you measure it, is your birthright. You have been commanded to be who you are — weird and wonderful, imperfect, messy, and lovely.

"...So be sure when you step. Step with care and great tact and remember that Life's a Great Balancing Act. Just never forget to be dexterous and deft..." —Dr. Seuss, *Oh, the Places You'll Go!*

PART 4
Success and Corporate America

Self-Awareness
+ Focus
+ Strategy
= **SUCCESS**

Chapter 15

Defining Success

"...And will you succeed? Yes! You will, indeed! (98 and ¾ percent guaranteed)." —Dr. Seuss, *Oh, the Places You'll Go!*

Here we are, finally all the concepts and nuances of personal mastery converge; we arrive at this destination called, "Success." Continue focusing on your vision for success and await Your Throne. Believe success is this assured. Let yourself trust your instincts and intuition. Your success is predicated on You! Life does not have to, nor was it intended to be energy draining! You were created to thrive, not only survive!

You have been hardwired to succeed; therefore, I invite you to boldly define what success feels and looks like for you. Resist the temptation to use external measurements in your definition of success, if you do, likely they will be at the expense of your own internal definition of success. However, your definition of success is way cooler and sexier than what the world tells you to pursue. Your definition of success is perfect and right because it comes from within you; extending from your personality, your personal values and your visions for success and sexiness.

Keep your eyes on the strengths and effortless behaviors of your silent influencers: your personality, keep the focus on your unique set of values for motivation, direction, and revenue opportunities! You are destined to succeed and your personality with its key defining value is what ensures it. Think, be creative, innovative, and results-focused: Sign up for the 4-week online course, "Self-Awareness for Success," receive a personality profile, exercises, and direction as to how you can confidently achieve successful transformation. Develop or claim your vision of success because it is within your reach! Believe the person you are has everything required to make that vision of success your reality! Enjoy the world on your terms. If it still feels too risky for you to move forward with such bold determination, identify what's holding you back. Determine how badly you want to progress and move forward.

Answer these two questions for yourself:
Question #1:
Does your life reflect the results you know you're capable of achieving?
Question #2:
Do you care enough to do something about it?

It's easy to intellectually tell yourself you care, if you really care, then do something about it. Anything. Success is cumulative, you just have to commit to making new, different, better choices. If you don't care, address that first. Go find something you can care about, or work with a coach to help you. You deserve to live a life of abundance, one that truly jazzes you, not just covers your expenses. Or, maybe you do what you do for the perks or the optics of it, but don't feel excited about what you're doing; either way, take action and do something about it!

Today, more than ever in this self-knowledge economy, you are set up to succeed. The world needs you to be excited about what you are working for and doing, and it is possible! Within your potential is the ability to have the maximum amount of personal success you desire.

Claiming Success

You've done the due diligence associated with personal success; you've taken the time to understand why who you are matters. You've begun to understand your success triggers, the strengths of your personality, and you've claimed a vision of success for yourself. Based on the anatomy of success and your own hardwiring, be assured you have everything it takes to claim your Throne as the Queen of You! The only ongoing effort required of you is to engage with the opportunities around you. An easy way to assess how, who, what, when, or where the opportunities could be, is via the Internet, assure yourself of the opportunities for your gain, everywhere. Actively engage in your exciting journey forward by applying your personal mastery: Your Vision of Success, Values, and Personality. Remember, *K.I.S.S.* is about keeping it simple, it isn't a complicated process, you can do this! You can get wherever you need to go. There are always options. You have to lead with an awareness of what you want, with creativity and boldness! Be grateful you have been hardwired to succeed. Embrace who you have been created to be and let your values direct you to your Throne! This isn't a "wish on a star" kind of encouragement or strategy, it is about applying strategic focus to your personal mastery. The best, most beautiful part of life—the part we don't trust—is that we're only responsible for the choices we make, and the way we treat others. We can choose in favor of the randomness of the world's strategy for success or we can choose to believe, trust, and know that our purpose and success come from within. Thrive, don't just survive.

Knowing Your Destiny & Purpose

My view on destiny and purpose is that it is achieved when we honor our potential and live life head-on, operating at our highest level of excellence!

As we deepen our personal awareness and personal understanding, we become active participants in the process of our own unfolding. As our visions for life, love and happiness evolve, and as we lead with our key defining values; we evolve into our destiny and purpose which is better and bigger than what we have been longing for.

> *"For I know the plans I have for you," declares the Lord, "plans to prosper you and not to harm you, plans to give you hope and a future." Jeremiah 29:11 (NIV)*

We live at the highest level of our excellence when we have alignment in our life. When there is harmony and flow between our being and doing, when there are shared values and shared visions for life in the work we do and/or with those with whom we journey; we have alignment. Be the beautiful, perfect, and wonderful woman you are. Symbolically, that means don't be willing to spend your day writing with your left hand, if you're naturally right-handed. Be more critical in your thinking before you get involved in a relationship with your opposite. While opposites attract and it can work, it is highly probable that it comes at the cost of someone's loss of potential. Remember, life is better when values and visions align, in life, and/or love. If you don't like the "Truth" of your essence and tell yourself you have to accept whatever jobs, or partners you can get, you're wrong. Invest in achieving personal mastery, and first ask your employer to cover your development tuition. Spend more time setting yourself up for success in life and love. Trust in your natural design and flow with it. It can be hard to do it on your own; call me, if you want some encouragement: 1–905–582–6030.

Each of the variables in the formula is of great consequence and they inform each other. For example, **Self-Awareness**, the starting point for **Focus**, on our values, enablers for personal excellence. **Focus** and **Self-Awareness** facilitate **Strategy** development enabling us to claim our visions of success. It's easy to balk at these simple words as we're generally told to take our cues from the outside-in. Except, we already know the outside-in approach doesn't work. Only you know the visions for success you have been created with, only you know how you want to feel. As uncomfortable as it may feel, there is no way around the truth that a leap of faith is required; *"leap and trust that the net will appear."* The more your objectives account for and capture your vision and values, the more assured your destiny of success!

Your full transformation *may* take longer than you were prepared for or wanted and you may feel tempted to say "screw it it's taking too long," or "I need the money NOW," or think faith in your thoughtful sophistication is enough…BUT, if you develop the habit of reacting in this way, or keep second-guessing yourself, it is quite likely you'll just end up saying "screw it" to your potential and say farewell to your Throne of Transformation. You are the Queen of you, and there would only be loss if you abdicated your Throne!

Choose from the strategies offered, or develop your own, stay committed to your Vision. Your success is contingent on your active engagement with the excellent adventure of your unfolding. Make it easier for yourself by signing up at www.mapforward.org/success, immediately get a profile of your personality, use our process, join the community of Queens like you, and begin to realize your destiny and potential.

Chapter 16

In Pursuit of Results

had a discussion with someone "today" about results and risk. He shared with me his personal story; essentially, he had left his family, job, language, and culture—everything familiar, behind in order to realize a better reality for him and his family.

"You're clearly a risk-taker," I said.

"No way," he said. "I keep my head down and just live my life."

While, on one hand, he acknowledged the huge risks he took to pursue his vision. He said he "wasn't a risk-taker, it was necessity which had driven him." Like Sally, he was operating from a reference point or misinformed sense of self that mostly only held him back. He very successfully tapped into and focused on his values of "vision," and "results," and minimized in his mind the risk he was taking. His approach worked, he stands by it today and he achieved his desired result; a better family and future for him and his family!

Share his story to highlight how we influence our own perceptions. We can tell ourselves we can't, or we can tell ourselves we can. We would be right in both examples. If you tell yourself you can't, you're right, you can't. When we tell ourselves "we can" and keep the focus on our desired results, leading with sexy values like "vision," "results," "courage"; inevitably, we will be met with a success, uncommon to most. I'm just conveying the promise which has been made to us all, by the Laws of the Universe and by God. *Both were in play before we got here. Let's stop fearing and be brave.*

When our values don't naturally align with what we are doing, success and results are evasive, we are less motivated and tend to disengage. To be successful, "results orientation" is required, and this is a developed skill. Develop this value for yourself and achieve a higher quality of life for yourself. Sometimes as women, we are not always comfortable pushing for results or leading with an overt results orientation. It is an unfortunate reality and a missed opportunity for both employer and employee. Employers could help more women develop their relationship and comfort with a "results-focused orientation." Help them learn how to reframe the unfamiliar and uncomfortable opportunities in their jobs. From a psychometric (behavioral science) perspective, 15% of the world is hardwired to directly comfortably pursue results. 85% of the world do not like to, nor easily do they do drive for results.

Evidence shows that all of us can make things happen and achieve results. The opportunity, therefore, is to empower the 85% who either don't know they could advance results in motivating ways and/or don't know how to comfortably push for results but would be open to learning "how" to ameliorate their relationship with "results." Some of us need to be shown, some of us need encouragement to believe in ourselves. Imagine the role, as an employer, you get to play in unleashing hidden potential! Empower more of your employees to push for results and confidently take calculated risks!

As it stands, we're always in pursuit of results. The pursuit of any desired reality(result), involves choosing in favor of opportunities, people, and jobs that will move us forward in powerful, meaningful, and success enabling ways. We are always making choices in our lives whether we do it knowingly or unknowingly, and we make choices in order to achieve specific outcomes, results. We tend to not give much thought to the "simple" results-focused choices we make like what to eat for dinner, or what to wear to work, or which route or mode of transport we will take to get to our destination. There are also the harder, heavier results-focused choices we make like who we want to be friends with, how to know the right partner, and whether or not to change jobs. Therefore, there are degrees of risk in each choice we make and if we want "more" because that is how progress is achieved, risk we must because the greatest hazard in life is to risk nothing, stay stuck in unfulfilling, potentially limiting status quos.

Choices and choosing are daily realities we all face. The more we embrace this truth, the more creative, and boldly curious we become about our decision-making strategies. The ability to choose is powerful and choosing is what enables each of us to influence the quality of our realities. The more aware we are of our personal values and the abilities within our personality the better positioned we are to progress. Progressing in life matters because *"there's more,"* say "yes" to your advancement. Each and every one of the choices we make shapes the quality of our experience; our life is always the sum total of our choices. For example, if there are aspects of your reality that you do not like, you may choose to do something about it to make it better, or you may not! Both choices will change the trajectory of your life in some profound way. It is easier to choose when we have an informed sense of what we are choosing in favor of: variations of the status quo, or progress. Both paths are encumbered with risk. As the Boss and Queen of you, comes the privilege and responsibility to actively and intentionally choose in favor of progress, joy, and success! As we increase our awareness, so too we increase the choices available to us, and as we develop our confidence and trust in ourselves, the better choices we make. Be more playful when considering your options, make more of your choices using growth-inducing values, and as your confidence grows and faith in this simple approach deepens, engage and develop some newer sexier values like risk, courage, creativity, and faith. This kind of boldness is really as simple as naming the values/feelings you want more of and then claiming them.

If that approach still feels unsafe for you, look for the evidence in your life of choices you've already successfully taken, small or big, daily or annually; take small steps or lead with your personal mastery and think big. Remember, you are hardwired to realize your visions with a strategy that will move you forward! Regardless of the challenges, or setbacks you may confront if you have a focused strategy, and lead with your personal mastery you will succeed!

You have been designed to succeed!

As you focus on your success, remember it's less about what life throws your way and more about how you choose to deal with and respond to those circumstances, that will dictate the outcome. Look beyond the pain of a tough situation and stay focused on your desired outcome. Choose to look at and react in more progressive, growth inducing ways; a positive response which enables self-development, growth, and learning. Engage in self-reflection more, focus on what you know to be true about your personality, your values, and your vision, but not in a passive, uh-huh, yep, I know—kind of way, but do this introspection with a commitment to living in flow with the immutable aspects of your excellence.

You are set up to succeed! The more consistently you follow the steps in *K.I.S.S.*, your career guide, the more assured your vision of success! Keep the focus on your transformation. If you do not yet have a transformation goal for yourself, give thought to an aspect of your life that you're unhappy with right now and answer these questions for yourself in your dedicated journal:

What about my current situation am I unhappy with?

What is my desired reality?

What are some changes that I can make now to move closer to my desired reality? For example, sign up for the 4-week online course, Self-Awareness for Success.

Self-awareness, thoughtful sophistication, or personal mastery, regardless of how you refer to it, with it, you have a firm foundation from which to make informed decisions and deal with life's challenges. The informed choices and risks you take will move you closer in meaningful, rewarding ways to your Throne. Acknowledge yourself for the courage you've shown in the choices you've made. Respect and embrace the unique ability of "risk tolerance" as it will move you forward and enable you to fill the space nature has allotted you! The sum of your choices dictates the direction and outcome of your life-keep choosing in favor of prosperity, fulfillment and joy! Embrace your potential. If you prefer to reframe your options in order to minimize how risky your options feel, that's entirely respectable, and has the potential to be powerful. Maintain focus on your vision for success. Choose big for your life; think progress, think growth, pursue excellence, sophistication, personal mastery, think success! Personal motivation comes from our key values. The more you can assure your "must-have" values are present, the more inspired and motivated you are. Test my proven thesis for yourself. Notice your results when your "must-have" values are present. Notice the areas of your life where you aren't engaged. It's a no-brainer! Sometimes we have to look for and claim the values/feelings we want, BUT, once we make this effort and find them, we are engaged and firing on all our cylinders. In the absence of inspiration and motivation, we disengage mentally. It is a very serious missed opportunity for employers and employees alike.

Ladies ask your employers to help you with this kind of personal development! Alignment is critical for high performance. Even with alignment, too many women aren't comfortable pushing for "results," a value. From a psychometric (behavioral science) perspective, 15% of the population are hardwired with this value and directly comfortably boldly pursue results, which means 85% of the population do not like to push too hard or are not comfortable having to drive for results in their lives. However, the truth is, we all consciously or unconsciously produce results, and each of us can make things happen to achieve more, better results. Another developmental opportunity is to enable the 85% who don't know how to access their ability to comfortably push for results. Some of us are required to have our potential shown to us directly. That was the case for me, I played small, held back and didn't know how to change my personal satisfaction with my life; UNTIL, I had my profile done, and explained to me. This stands to be a potential game changer for your employees as well. Imagine what your company has to gain by empowering more of your employees to embrace and pursue results! It is not at all uncommon to require validation and assurance before embarking on new opportunities. With the focus on results, it is easier to manage risks, and the more risks we take, the better we get at finding new, different results to pursue and risks to take.

Chapter 77

The Self-Knowledge Economy

t's generally accepted that we're living in a *"knowledge economy."* Fritz Machlup, an Austrian-American economist, was among the first to examine *knowledge as an economic resource.* Peter Drucker later popularized the concept. Basically, they say, there are two types of workers in the knowledge economy: manual workers who work with their hands to produce goods or services and knowledge workers who work with their heads and produce ideas, knowledge, and information.

My take on their concept is only slightly different, I say: We live in a self-knowledge economy, and the most important kind of knowledge to have as an economic resource, is self-knowledge (thoughtful sophistication). Self-knowledge workers are the most successful, whether their success is with their hands, or with their content knowledge. The ROI of a wholesale *self-knowledge* approach will always be in direct proportion to an individual's *self-knowledge*, aka, *self-awareness*, aka, *thoughtful sophistication*, aka, *personal mastery*; a somewhat vague and airy-fairy approach. Except, in a self-knowledge economy, the most strategic investment, is one that directly and immediately, empowers the individual. Therefore, the business case is obvious: "What's good for the employee, is good for the company."

"Self-knowledge" is an economic resource and those who have it are more content, successful, and productive for themselves and for their employers. While the obviousness of the logic is abundant, the workplace emphasis remains on variables such as education, contacts, and lucky breaks. While aptitudes, education, and lucky breaks can enhance our personal fulfillment and satisfaction, it's not a given. These variables do not always translate into high performance or satisfaction for employer or employee; at best they guarantee a 50–50 chance of success.

The invisible drivers-personality, personal values and visions of success will always be the most powerful variables which dictate the quality of our lives! It can be no other way, try as we might to dismiss these truths. Employers and employees deserve better odds than 50–50, and while it may be viewed as an inconvenient hassle for those who lack emotional intelligence, it is very strategic to do a reset with a willingness to endure some short term "pain" for long term gain. Perhaps, this is amongst the opportunities this global pandemic provides employers with, to be more strategic about their growth strategies and profit vis a vis their people. It's too tempting for companies to be like kids, with eyes bigger than their stomachs. Growth, if achievable, is not sustainable if employees are not aligned and the "eggs are in the wrong basket"; mental health, productivity, and business results suffer. How often would the reverse order apply; pour tons of money into hiring a bunch of randomly selected educated people and then pour tons of money in search of a business opportunity?

It is in the best long-term interest of Presidents and CEOs to consider different, new kinds of due diligence and action initiatives which factor in and account for the true needs of its' employees. It is clearly time to accept that companies are people first and it's never going back to how things were. Though employers provide employees with a paycheque, individuals work to live, not live to work; therefore, companies are now second or third. Times have changed. Companies that don't keep up with their workforce, we already know, get left behind. Personal development and self-awareness are mentally engaging owing to high performance. The heightened awareness, understanding, and enhanced performance of thoughtful sophistication, personal mastery is a competitive advantage for individuals and for their employers. When self-knowledge is not advanced or supported, employers run the avoidable likely risk of mediocre performance from their employees without either ever even knowing how much more potential the employee had to give. Disenfranchised employees, either quit or worse, they don't and continue to work though disengaged.

Chapter 18

The Business Case

As Jim Collins writes in, Good to Great, people impact the success of EVERYTHING. An organization has at least 6 clear opportunities to generate tangible returns just by advancing self-awareness/thoughtful sophistication/personal mastery.

1. There are frequent examples in the media of lawsuits, costly avoidable blithes due to negligence, carelessness, or incompetence related to **misalignment** between employees and the jobs they perform. Just as people have personalities so do jobs. The more aligned the two personalities, job, and individual, are to each other the better the returns for a company in every way: lower absenteeism, more motivated and productive employees, and less turnover. Alignment is operational efficiency. A self-knowledge economy works best when leaders, not just Human Resource

(H.R) professionals, know their people at an in-depth level and not only from externally informed sources (education and performance reviews) or biased input (interviews, and bosses' personal perspective). Leaders are required to lead. The privilege of leadership is responsibility, and it is the responsibility of the Leaders, not just H.R, to ensure all employees, not just the top 10% of them, are firing on all their cylinders. An operational win/win! Of course, doing so would be an onerous undertaking for leaders with their own deliverables. Thankfully, none of us has to do it alone and other external resources like MaP Forward Inc. exist to help address the chasm that may exist between where employees currently are in their development and how they wish their desired reality could be. The business case for this kind of development is undeniable.

2. The very real palpable opportunity in a #MeToo era is to actively care about female empowerment. Do a reset, change the discussions and options you provide your female employees in order to positively impact their productivity. The #MeToo movement isn't going away, instead, it is bringing the issues women face, very squarely and acutely, into present-day awareness. There is no question that harassment, in all its subtle forms, impedes progress for the employer and the employee. The business case for this kind of development is undeniable.

3. During the hard times of COVID-19, especially, while most companies are working remotely, the very real strategic, motivating, and empowering opportunity is to offer every employee, who wants it, guided self-development. The business case is for investment in focused personal employee development. Employees learn how to embrace their personal excellence in order to be better, more productive, engaged, and motivated. This kind of strategic inside out awareness and development highlights for

each individual employee their available options for positive impact upon others, and the overall output of the teams they belong to. Although remote work has been stressful and isolating for many employees and challenging for employers, it also presents opportunities like this, to think outside of the box, and offer employees direct sustainable pathways to personal mastery, which includes Emotional Intelligence (EQ). Emotional Intelligence is defined as the ability to comprehend and manage personal emotions while simultaneously understanding the emotions of others. The shift to more remote work has produced changes for both employees and employers which makes EQ even more vital, however, it is harder to achieve without self-awareness, personal mastery, thoughtful sophistication. EQ is about values, a core concept in personal mastery. Personal values are the silent and invisible influencers that few actually understand, and as such EQ is often dismissed and overlooked. However, now, in remote work environments, the personal values of each employee are what dictate their level of engagement and productivity on a daily basis! While values can feel like a nebulous concept for both employees and employers when consciously incorporated, they are actually meaningful, results-oriented, and relationship enabling conduits.

The personal values we each have are our unique and specific set of success triggers, the more our key values are present the better our results. The more we learn to know and understand our success triggers, the more naturally we look for opportunities to incorporate them into our work and achieve better results! Unfortunately, most of us don't know HOW to lead with our values, and instead, personal satisfaction is hit or miss.

4. With the advent of remote work as a daily reality, the more employees are empowered to understand the dynamics at play in their own performance as well as the performance of their

team members, the easier it is to feel connected and engaged with each other. Most employees don't realize that their personal values, which often differ from the values of those they work with, are their unique and specific success triggers. To not account for the invisible influence of your employees' values, success triggers is a missed opportunity that comes at the expense of profit: lower engagement, motivation, and performance. It's okay if the thought of offering this kind of holistic development for your employees is a new and different approach to professional development, it's time for a reset. Employees are facing challenges amid a pandemic and a massive economic contraction and even the most emotionally intelligent amongst your employees are faced with serious challenges posed by the current crisis. The related isolation is a daily reality for millions of employees, and many of their challenges could be addressed, with corporate-sponsored online development, *"Self-Awareness for Success."*

Investment in this process produces results, brings fulfillment, and delivers success. People never reach their limits…they only think they do; help your employees understand and know the depth and breadth of their potential! The business case for providing employees with informed, objective self-understanding that enables greater satisfaction, higher levels of performance, and better results is undeniable. It is in the best interest of employers to ensure their employees are motivated, engaged, and set up to succeed!

The more individuals can understand and find personal meaning and purpose in the work they are doing, the better their ability to clearly communicate and express needs to their boss and team members. This kind of investment in individual personal development has a direct impact on the bottom-line through increased output and engagement. The business case for this kind of development is undeniable.

The new generations of employees, millennials, specifically are an incredibly diverse generation. The diversity and vulnerability of this cohort is a reality that deserves innovative, unique, cost-effective, support, and development processes. Recent polls reveal that millennials, of different backgrounds, have high anxiety around how the coronavirus will affect their economic realities and career opportunities. Help them learn to play the long game, empower them with a competitive advantage that enables them to always stand strong, and chart their own course. The necessity of remote work, team deliverables, self-motivation, and self-discipline requires a whole new approach to achieving results and boosting productivity. The current crisis is a forced opportunity for CEO's to get more involved with the developmental offerings of its organization and promote profit with purpose! The business case for this kind of development is undeniable.

5. **Team Building**, Corporations, and businesses of all sizes are required to meet the needs and expectations of these new generations of employees, otherwise, they may quit, disengage from their work and deliver only mediocre results. With so many employees, most of whom are unfamiliar with what they have to leverage or how they could leverage the potential of their personalities, now working remotely and in teams, businesses have a new set of nuances to respond to. The opportunity is to be more creative about support offerings. One size has never fit all, though we have the same shared objectives and want to feel engaged, motivated, and productive. Remote work environments present challenges that require addressing, little about this new normal is easy, or obvious, but it is clear that team success deserves and needs support. The business case for this kind of development is undeniable.

6. **Self-Awareness, thoughtful sophistication, personal mastery** is transformative, and indispensable in the workplace. With it,

employees do better more targeted self-care, develop stronger communication skills, and learn how to address and improve upon their fundamental interpersonal and emotional needs.

It may not seem like Self-Awareness would be relevant at a time when individuals are working remotely and the need for in-person interactions has fallen off drastically, but the opposite is true. Existing problems such as a lack of engagement have only been exacerbated by the transition to remote work. Too many employees feel alienated which makes it more difficult for them to do their jobs and some experience harmful psychological consequences. Increased self-understanding enables superior results, including the ability for employees to take control of their work environments. Leaders can be more innovative in order to forge better agreements with their employees; the paycheque is not enough to foster loyalty or make them feel empowered. Tap into new resources that celebrate individual strengths, uniqueness, and enable the communication of new innovative ideas. Point more of your employees and consumers towards innovation and new solutions - reward the employees who seek progressive powerful changes and improvements for a more fulfilling status quo. Help your employees by providing them with access to personal mastery so they know how they can conquer and move past their status quo. Too many of your employees and consumers feel alone and helpless. Let them know you understand, care, and take action by providing them with self-awareness for success. Personal mastery is a very strategic and empowering concept that enables personal leadership and know-how to address needs and concerns. The business case for this kind of development is undeniable.

Chapter 19
The Purpose Economy

We are in a new economy; the World Economic Forum has termed it the "purpose economy." Throughout history, the tide of economic development has expanded and changed the way life, on all fronts, is approached. Present-day awareness is what determines the direction of the future for companies and individuals alike.

Today it seems, the collective desire is to evolve the relationship between work and wealth. More companies, for that reason, are starting to care about "meaning creation" for their stakeholders, employees, and consumers. Regardless of business or industry, the company's employees are drawn to, are the ones that can give them "increase in life."

K.I.S.S. is specifically focused on women, and for companies progressive and smart enough to offer "increase in life," to this advancing group.

"Meaning creation" is about purpose. "Increase in life," is about advancement, specifically, the kind of advancement that women have been patiently waiting for. Women are ready to capitalize on the tides of change the #MeToo era has ushered in. Women who choose to work, or are required to, want to feel that their lives are getting better because of their work, not worse. When work only offers a paycheque, too many of your employees are just showing up for the steady paycheque, or worse, not showing up but still getting the paycheque. Your stakeholders; employees, consumers, and shareholders, likely, care about the standards, approaches, and compassion of the companies with whom they, work, support, and invest. The onus is on the corporate world to better address the wants of its employees and consumers.

In the purpose economy, the reset is towards a more rational model based around *self-knowledge*. Without this kind of support offering for employees and consumers, the likelihood is that too many disengage from life, mentally. We all want more of something: progress, success, or fulfillment. We all want lives with an inspiring purpose; we are all hardwired with a shared desire for meaning. Companies are uniquely able to help advance these pursuits in meaningful ways. Yet, unfortunately, too many employers tolerate knowing employees are mostly only bringing their school-based education, with no real sense of self to inform them about how they can deliver higher performance. Imagine the costs in productivity, flow, and profit, when employees don't know what, or how to leverage their personality, and only bring their technical skills, aptitudes, or education!

How is that a reliable business model?...

Especially when it is so easy to enable your employees to be better! Provide your employees AND consumers access to a credible, proven online process that advances and supports personal understanding. It's priced to be accessible and affordable for any employer or woman who wants a competitive advantage. Unless women, as a whole, are shown how to understand their personality, values, and success triggers, too many women risk not realizing their purpose, the new economic driver. The world and your company are losing the available drive and motivation that exists—leaving money on the table.

The emphasis in this Purpose Economy includes personal mastery, for purpose. We have a whole generation of individuals who have grown up in the information age. They have an intrinsic bias for data, and information and have unlimited access to it. However, as we all know, not everything we have access to is of equal value. For information to be reliably trusted by this demographic their discerning minds accept information that comes from credible, substantiated sources, and when the conclusions have been arrived at with sufficient due diligence. This is a good strategy when learning about things "out there." However, in this new economic era, the driving engine is purpose, and the most strategic, empowering information is not "out there," it is from within, where the pursuits are less tangible, but from where all results originate. Quests for purpose and meaning, are results every individual is striving for. They are feeling based objectives: Unique, personal information which only comes from within. However, with an intrinsic bias for external information, finding purpose and meaning by looking within is not so obvious. Instead, it becomes a more elusive pursuit in the absence of knowing what to look for, and how to make it relevant for success and satisfaction. The journey to an inspiring, motivating mission, is harder and takes longer to achieve without guided development. Consider all the individual potential that risks being left untapped, if not aided. While this kind of support may not be what all of your employees seek and want, it is undoubtedly, a very welcome option/offer for the countless employees who do. An operational and business win: win.

Corporate "America" is uniquely poised to help these individuals. Working with more and more Millennials willing and eager to find their purpose, it has become clear to me, few know how to start such a process, or what questions to ask to get the purpose process started. Many corporations are already actively taking steps to advance this purpose economy by enabling their employees to feel more empowered and inspired to bring their best to the job. Unfortunately, many Corporations, are not.

An easy option, for companies already using personality assessments in their hiring process, is to give each employee, hired or not, their report with a disclaimer. Be like Santa in Miracle on 34th street. Don't only want to help them if they work for you, send them on their way with access to insights they might otherwise never receive! Enable as many of your consumers and employees as you can to grow from the inside out, while honoring their intrinsic bias for information and data.

More outside in approaches are not what is most needed, though it may be all employees know to ask for or want. Instead, offer them access to useful, strategic, insights about their potential and strengths. To not, leaves too many employees feeling empty, minimized, disengaged, frustrated, and demotivated. If companies don't help these employees, who will? Much of each day is spent at the employers' place of business; in that way, work has a certain implied level of responsibility like parents and schools once had. Employees of all ages, consciously or unconsciously, but rightfully so, look to their employers to help them grow and advance.

Disengaged employees are a drag on the output of entire nations. Too much misalignment between people and the roles they assume is being tolerated contributing to this disengagement. Performance reviews already show that education and technical skills are not enough to be motivated to do a job well. Both people and jobs have personality traits, and the closer the alignment of the two, the better the returns for a company, in every way.

Reset: Create Purpose

Businesses that enable purpose for their employees ultimately, win. As utopian as it may sound, there is evidence in almost every industry and throughout our culture that this shift is already underway. Enable women to advance professionally and personally. Enable them to know "how to" cross the chasm between where they are and where they want to be; and you won't have to. It is relatively easy to do, and fundamental in advancing the purpose economy amongst your workforce. Unless an employee is enabled to understand their potential, the odds of them disengaging from work without a sense of purpose or meaning, in general, is much higher. Companies lose with lower productivity and higher turnover: Employees lose the opportunity for increased engagement and self-satisfaction: the world risks losing unrealized potential. While this is especially true for generations, X, Y, and Z, the same rationale stands true for all of us, at any age, who want to be part of the solution for a better world, not part of the problem associated with unrealized potential.

When considered in the context of size, Millennials, Gen Y's, represent the future of the entire labor force. Many are already taking on leadership roles, others not. Neither of these two groups knows nor understands the full breadth of their potential, leaving it mostly untapped; reducing your potential returns in productivity and profit. The high levels of turnover, absenteeism, lower productivity, and lack of motivation are all signs from this new workforce that it's time for a reset. You have a unique, vital opportunity to shape a better world, by shaping more women, from the inside-out.

Trends

Brain sizes have increased, and as a result, "more" is required for people to reach their full potential. Self-development and mindfulness are critical aspects of a meaningful and fulfilling life and career. It is a time of unprecedented growth for personal development, people want hope and direction to enhance their own growth.

Be a "Company that Cares," not just by saying the words, but by helping your stakeholders improve the quality of their lives. Research shows that most employees don't expect utopian experiences; they only want incrementally better lives, in meaningful ways. Unfortunately, the gap between people's expectations and what companies offer is enormous. Hence why the newer generation of employees, especially, tend to be indifferent to their employer.

Chapter 20

#MeToo and #Microed,
Micro-aggressive Sexual Harassment

"Microaggression" is a term that was coined by Harvard professor Chester M. Pierce back in the 1970s to describe the constant onslaught of offenses that black people experience in their day-to-day interactions with white people. Columbia psychology professor Derald Wing Sue, later expanded the concept to include its effects on other marginalized groups, including women. Microaggressions are the more subtle slights that may occur daily for people from diverse communities, backgrounds, and identities. Because of the delicate nature of these slights, they are hard to identify or "prove" and tend to get unaddressed, enabled, and tolerated.

Let's use the #microed as the gathering hashtag for the issue of microaggressive sexual harassment: a less obvious, and more subtle form of sexual harassment. The fact, that many women are #microed, is not "new"; it's just that historically, these types of aggressions have been over-looked, and or, allowed for. For too long, women have had to be on the defensive and just tolerate being #microed. It is safe to say that there is not a single woman who isn't relieved that companies are now also on the defensive. During this age of reckoning, there is a growing realization of the challenges marginalized groups, contend with. The right to increase for all must be defended.

We, women, who have been #microed know how real the damages they cause, are. Micro aggressive acts are not as blatant as "in your face" discrimination or sexual assault as #MeToo violations, but they are more prevalent. #Microed issues have a dark and damaging cumulative effect, a slow form of torture like "death by a thousand cuts": None of the inflic-tions are fatal in themselves, they add up and cause a slow and painful demise of our sense of self-worth, amongst other damages.

In Chapter 4, I share my #microed, #MeToo story. It was a function of a blatant power imbalance: A powerful CEO, in a powerful company and an influential top producer in the business. He was not held account-able for his #microed actions, despite their policy.

They bullied me with their coercive power and leverage. Mr. CEO's highly influential and "unavoidable" presence within the business com-munity, at large, made this #microed issue impossible to overcome as a self-employed professional, required to be seen as above reproach. What kind of protection are you offering your female independent service pro-viders, do you provide them a better avenue to voice abuses, even at the Executive level?

Watch Dogs

Corporations can defend and protect marginalized groups who are #microed by appointing an individual from each of the marginalized groups, as a watchdog. Their responsibility could be to bring these issues to light, not to render a conclusion of culpability, but to demand account-ability. Marginalized vulnerable groups deserve the added protection of a watchdog. Otherwise, when a member of the Executive branch is required to police one of their own leaders, they tend to find themselves in a no-win situation. Decisions or choices made in this conflicted posi-tion, risk being unjust. The Chairman of the Board has a vested interest in silencing those who speak up, especially when he is recognized as an Independent' Chair?? Board members have too many of their own exter-nal distractions to want to let such issues surface, drag on, or have to be confronted. Each of these individuals, though in positions of power with influence, have their own agenda. The current model is an inconsistent and unreliable model to deliver justice and effectively address such out-side disruptions. Having lived the experience, I have no illusions about how #microed harassment issues can play out within a multinational cor-poration which presumably holds itself to higher standards. In my case, it was dismissed by an entire branch of executives in a well-reputed global company: not just by the Chairman, or the VP of Human Resources, or the Head of Legal, or the VP of Communications, or existing CEO, or the young female board member who inherited her company from her father and is now the President at her own global mining company, but also the incoming President. All of these professionals dismissed com-pany policy and the #microed substantiated claim for the unfair reasons they did. Had the damages not been so severe, the Chairman may have offered me a nice $100 G, kept it away from the shareholders, and sent me on my way with a nondisclosure agreement. I share my story with the hope of increasing awareness of such #microed behaviors. These kinds of moral and ethical injustices are not one-offs, they are merely toler-ated and not considered serious enough issues though they are a form of sexual harassment.

#Microed individuals impact workplace profitability through many factors; such as reduced productivity, absenteeism, turnover, health, well-being, and lower morale. These variables directly impact shareholders' financial returns. Socially responsible investors may react to such violations if they are aware, so the most natural option for Boards is to do nothing, lest the shareholders become aware and those with daughters, actively react. When there can be no assurance of ethical and moral decision making at the top of any company, who is actually protecting the vulnerable employees at the lower levels since history has shown that Human Resources may not. Justice can never be achieved when it exists on a very muddy, slippery slope, companies must be more progressive, and compassionate. Attention can no longer only be given to blatant expressions of discrimination or harassment, microaggressions in all its manifestations can no longer be tolerated, overlooked, and dismissed. The standards we hold each other to in life must be rigorously applied within companies: Zero tolerance for unethical and immoral behavior.

If any of you have been #Microed and feel like your complaints and efforts for justice have been ignored, feel free to contact me. I'm not a lawyer, however, I swam with the sharks, learned much, and exist to use my voice to help others. I'd be happy to try and help you achieve justice, pending no conflict of interest.

Chapter 27

MaP Forward Inc.
(MaP = Mastery and Purpose) and the
MaP Forward University

The MaP Forward University offers a 4-week online course, "Self-Awareness for Success," the first transformational offering of its kind: www.mapforward.org/success. *K.I.S.S.* is the companion guide for this highly exclusive offering. We are a unique, globally proven effective, easy to access, strategic, and cost-effective process founded on a for profit model. Outsource your developmental needs to us, now a Government of Canada, registered, non-profit. Give your employees, teams, and consumers access to our course, with 4 modules and an interactive session, each week. Our offering is a proven effective process that builds on solid evidence of adult learning and growth patterns (see examples below): We offer expert coaching/facilitation and model for our participants how to be real, courageous, challenging, provocative, and vulnerable. Embedded within our community-based model is peer learning which magnifies the impact of personal mastery, thoughtful sophistication, self-awareness. We learn best from our own experiences, but peer learning is also useful and supportive relationships are developed, another longer-term ROI of our process.

Offer our program to employees working remotely, encourage your stakeholders to access the course as a daily pattern interrupt for added motivation and empowerment; enable them to return to their "to-do's" more aware, focused, and engaged! Your employees/teams receive access to scientifically valid and reliable AI technology, a psychometric assessment, which profiles each employee using the 7 personality traits established by science, as most impacting results professionally and personally. They also receive a report that shows them their alignment with their job and what behaviors they could choose to develop or learn, along with other helpful tools and assignments. An added benefit for participants is membership within our exclusive online Facebook community for added support. At the end of the 4-week program, each participant receives a Certificate of Completion, and the hours even apply as unverified professional development! *Self-Awareness for Success* is a convenient and cost-effective process for high performance, and also makes available professional coaching services for those who want to better direct their personalities to realize more rewarding results! As an online offering, *Self-Awareness for Success* is a very cost-effective offering for all your stakeholders: consumers and employees. In times of crisis especially, professional development that empowers the individual is an investment that produces many returns, including confidence-building, loyalty and helps maintain a team spirit that directly influences the short- and long-term engagement and productivity of your company.

Learning and Development Principles Built Into MaP Forward Inc.

1. Personal Development = Professional Success

The research shows that

Awareness of self (values, personality, etc.)

+ awareness of others (their values, personality, etc.)

+ awareness of the impact the self has on others

+ ability to regulate our emotions and actions relative to the desired objectives

= **More success in life and work**

2. Individuals learn best using the 70/20/10 rule

There is a whole body of evidence for the 70/20/10 rule (Centre for Creative Leadership)

http://www.ccl.org/wp-content/uploads/2015/04/
    BlendedLearningLeadership.pdf

Learning is 70% about having challenging experiences that cause learning and growth

+ 20% developmental relationships, bosses, mentors, coaches, and social learning with peers

+ 10% specific models, tools, lessons, etc.

Our program continually challenges and encourages participants to go after challenging assignments, and opportunities that enable, promote, and cause growth. We operate with a developmental coaching relationship and a developmental peer network.

Why Us?

MaP Forward Inc. exists in order to provide employees and consumers personal advancement that increases their professional success. Neither group may, otherwise, have the opportunity to receive sophisticated output that is useful, relevant, objective, and personally accurate at a deep level. Who knows how participants will direct their personal master, thoughtful sophistication, self-awareness, perhaps it will be for the betterment of the world, or maybe as some version of the next Amelia Earhart!

Benefits of the MaP Forward "University"

When companies employ initiatives that make their stakeholders lives "better," they, in turn, realize increased loyalty, access new customers, and deepen their relationships with the stakeholders. A Market Watch trend has identified "A strong majority (91 percent) of consumers and employees want brands/companies to assist them in realizing their personal goals." Be amongst the early adopters, offer what the market is seeking.

Specifically, offer this service for the women in your organization and consumer base.

MaP Forward Inc. is uniquely poised to satisfy the shift in the marketplace for more self-help. Sponsoring companies and companies that make the MaP Forward University available to their employees and consumers have a unique opportunity to truly differentiate themselves. A cause-related marketing effort that gives back to your stakeholders. Sponsoring companies have unlimited access to our university, for their stakeholders; *employees and consumers*; change lives in positive ways, at no additional cost to you.

It's simple: Empower and enable women to realize the fullness of their potential. Help them to know how to feel and be more productive. Invite them to find their voice, speak up and out. Minimize your #microed and #MeToo complaints.

Women want to know "how to" cross the chasms facing them, and MaP Forward Inc. is here to help you, help them.

MaP Forward Inc.

Sheeba Forbes is the founder and Executive Director of MaP Forward Inc. Before that, her focus was as President of Forward Focus™ Inc. (FFI) a Global Executive Coaching firm that used a proven and well-known innovative personality enhancing AI technology. As an accomplished executive life coach, published author, media personality (TV and radio), and international keynote speaker, her firm's clients have been drawn from global, public and private business, municipalities, charities, and foundations as well as with private clients interested in accessing more of their potential. The AI, assessment technology we've been using for two decades, is state of the art, scientifically valid, and reliable.

MaP Forward Inc. now directs the same proven unique value proposition (UVP), including technology, to the female consumer market. The mission of MaP Forward Inc. is advanced through public speaking and a multi-media platform of courses and webinars.

The emphasis is on education, empowerment, and encouragement:

Self-Awareness + Focus + Strategy = Success

I end *K.I.S.S.* with Bhatsy's story, and Part 4 of my story:

Meet Bhatsy

Bhatsy, who graduated at the top of her class, was a valued millennial with high potential and in an excellent job with a good company. She had every reason to expect she would feel great for it. Except, she didn't feel great, and couldn't understand why. Options she considered: change companies, get another degree, suck it up, and continue delivering mediocre results, "nobody even paid attention."

She didn't know what to do, and to add to that she didn't feel confident in voicing her preferences to her male bosses.... "Getting another job may be better," that's what her friend Erika did. "But she wasn't really satisfied with that company either."

Bhatsy is naturally hardwired to realize results and be proactive but didn't own it, because she couldn't imagine herself that way. All she knew was that she was bored. The "perfect storm" was brewing because of her lack of self-understanding, in a company with managers too busy for her, and stories about other friends just bolting for similar reasons were all coming to a climax.

Fact: In the absence of knowing how and where she could excel, she stopped trying.

Bhatsy's company was a highly successful multinational. Her CEO was introduced to MaP Forward Inc. by our Chairman. This CEO knew of my flagship client, and upon learning that the same proven process was being offered to millennials, at not-for-profit pricing—he offered it to Bhatsy as well as almost two dozen other millennial employees in his company. Testimonials are available on the course landing page: www.mapforward. org/success. Pleased with the response and results we were generating, he offered it to his three well-educated kids and even spoke to his friends about it and they enrolled their kids! The CEO got involved in this initiative because his company was having too much turnover, shareholders didn't like it and his executive were complaining about low productivity and motivation. Then, he was introduced to MaP Forward Inc., and me.

Bhatsy cringed after seeing her assessment, realizing how much she was limiting herself professionally. She accepted the science behind her profile (intrinsic bias). The contents of her report resonated deeply. Privately, she had already wondered about her potential, and if some of the things she was reading were really possible for her. Bhatsy's confidence and motivation grew she tried being more vocal in her department and tried to seize more of the opportunities she noticed. Unfortunately for both the company and Bhasty, she couldn't get the support she needed from her manager and decided to move on.

Most organizations have "Bhatsy" situations: keen, underperforming, unmotivated, ignored, misaligned with the company, and role; employees unsure of how to bring about change in the direction of growth.

Self-awareness is the determining variable in the formula because, without it, too many key outcomes are a crapshoot, dependent on education, and technical skills being enough. An employee may stay if they feel supported, or they may leave to find better alignment. Attrition, in general, is a good thing. When a dissatisfied employee leaves, the company can find someone who is a better fit, more aligned with a manager's plan for the role.

Unfamiliar conversations for sure: but that's ok: it's time for a reset.

Part 4

The Investigators the multinational hired asked me how this could be "resolved."

1. *I asked that the global company be a sponsor of MaP Forward Inc.*
2. *I requested stock options for my son and daughter and*
3. *Told them they could decide what a fair settlement would be, now fully aware of the damages they had caused my career, and mental health.*

My requests for restoration were dismissed outright. I understand. A large settlement would have to be accounted for and recorded in the Annual Report, Shareholders may ask questions and potentially react. The Independent Chairman wrote to me that if I went public, they would bury me in legal fees.

"…So be sure when you step. Step with care and great tact and remember that Life's a Great Balancing Act. Just never forget to be dexterous and deft.…"

…And will you succeed? Yes! You will, indeed! (98 and ¾ percent guaranteed.)." —Dr. Seuss, *Oh, the Places You'll Go!*

CALL TO ACTION

end this book with a call to action for your company, form a strategic alliance with MaP Forward Inc., we exist to educate, encourage, and empower women.

1. Enable your employees to cultivate their self-awareness and understand their potential. www.mapforward.org/success is an overview of the 4-week online course offered through the MaP Forward University.

2. Revise existing paradigms, place purpose alongside profit. Doing so will shift more attention to the needs of each woman in your workforce inspiring them with their own potential for better results.

3. Advance the Purpose Economy, do a reset in your company: satisfy the desires amongst your workforce for an increased sense of purpose and meaning creation.

MaP Forward Inc is a "not only, but also" value proposition that is high tech and high touch, face-to-face but remote, an intuitive and high energy process that reaffirms to participants who they are and then invites them to step into it, rock their future. We transfer knowledge and engage in dialogue for self-discovery and high performance. We are a cost-effective great investment, that is about personal mastery.

I encourage CEO's, Human Resources, and Training & Development professionals to offer this proven process as a resetting value add, now. The business case for this kind of development is undeniable. There will always be a direct correlation between high-performance, success and self-understanding. When we know-how and what we have to leverage, we are able to then leverage the fullness of our personality and perform better. In the absence of support that enables personal understanding and strategic actions, results tend to reflect a hit or miss strategy—frustration and demotivation for the employer and the employee.

ABOUT THE AUTHOR

have been a professionally certified Executive Life Coach for the past two decades. Before that, I earned a Bachelor of Arts degree from Wilfrid Laurier University, and majored in French and Psychology, with a minor in Business. I lived abroad in my senior year of high school, as a Rotary Exchange student, and have been bilingual in French/English, ever since.

Professionally, I have been blessed with international, national, and regional media attention, and worked with some of the most influential businessmen in Canada, as an Executive Life Coach. I was on the Prime Minister of Canada's Task Force for Women Entrepreneurs and nominated as amongst the Top 40 Under 40 in Canada, for my business success. I am a tv/radio personality and published author. My first book, *Sheeba's Secret*, is available in bookstores across North America, and I am also an international keynote speaker. Now, as the Founder and Executive Director of MaP Forward Inc., a government registered not-for-profit, I am focused on empowering, educating, and encouraging women. *K.I.S.S. (Keep it Simple & Sexy): The Career Guide for Women* Unwilling to Compromise, my second book, is available globally in bookstores and airports around the world.

I have excelled in my life and career despite a #MeToo, #Microed story which derailed my successful entrepreneurial path. Raised by men, a forceful father, and 4 brothers, my sense of reality has always been a tad skewed. Like Tarzan, I am most comfortable with "Apes." My natural ease with men along with my strong results-focused personality has made CEOs and Senior Executives, my natural target audience. Then.

Now, I share my unique process, vantage points, insights, knowledge, and professional expertise, with women who want "more."

A free ebook edition is available with the purchase of this book.

To claim your free ebook edition:

1. Visit MorganJamesBOGO.com
2. Sign your name CLEARLY in the space
3. Complete the form and submit a photo of the entire copyright page
4. You or your friend can download the ebook to your preferred device

Morgan James
BOGO™

A **FREE** ebook edition is available for you or a friend with the purchase of this print book.

CLEARLY SIGN YOUR NAME ABOVE

Instructions to claim your free ebook edition:
1. Visit MorganJamesBOGO.com
2. Sign your name CLEARLY in the space above
3. Complete the form and submit a photo of this entire page
4. You or your friend can download the ebook to your preferred device

Print & Digital Together Forever.

Snap a photo

Free ebook

Read anywhere

CPSIA information can be obtained
at www.ICGtesting.com
Printed in the USA
JSHW031941161221
21308JS00001B/16